The Odyssey

Homer

Level 4

Retold by Fiona Beddall

Series Editors: Andy Hopkins and Jocelyn Potter

Pearson Education Limited

Edinburgh Gate, Harlow,
Essex CM20 2JE, England
and Associated Companies throughout the world.

ISBN: 978-1-292-14052-0

This edition first published by Pearson Education Ltd 2008

1 3 5 7 9 10 8 6 4 2

Text copyright © Pearson Education Ltd 2008
Illustrations by Marcelo Sosa
The author has asserted her moral right in accordance with the
Copyright Designs and Patents Act 1988

Set in 11/13pt A. Garamond
Printed in China
SWTC/01

Produced for the Publishers by AC Estudio Editorial S.L.

Published by Pearson Education Ltd.

For a complete list of the titles available in the Pearson English Active Readers series, visit www.pearsonenglishactivereaders.com.
Alternatively, write to your local Pearson Education office or to
Pearson English Readers Marketing Department, Pearson Education, Edinburgh Gate, Harlow, Essex CM20 2JE, England.

Contents

1.1 What's the book about?

This book is about a man's journey home from the Trojan War. What do you think? Circle the correct words.

1 The hero's name is *Odysseus / Achilles*.

2 He is *Egyptian / Greek*.

3 He lived *more than 3,000 / about 1,000* years ago.

4 His return has been delayed by *bad weather / the gods*.

1.2 What happens first?

Look at these pictures and answer the questions. What do you think?

1 Who are the people? Write 1–4.

a ☐ the hero's son

b ☐ the hero's wife

c ☐ the hero's servant

d ☐ a man who wants to marry the hero's wife

2 Guess the answers to these questions. Write 1–4.

a ☐ ☐ Which two people love Odysseus completely?

b ☐ Which person wants Odysseus to return but is upset with him?

c ☐ Which person doesn't want him to return?

CHAPTER 1

An Island without a King

'If you prefer to destroy my property, then stay. But I will ask Zeus for a day of judgement, and on that day I will destroy you.'

'Odysseus's unlucky **fate** is causing me great sadness,' said the goddess Athene to her father, the great god Zeus. 'It is now twenty years since he has seen his home and loving family. Zeus, Father, King of Kings, why are you doing nothing to help this man?'

'I have not forgotten the great hero Odysseus, my child,' replied Zeus. 'You are right – his troubles have continued long enough. We should bring him home.'

'Thank you, Father,' said bright-eyed Athene. 'First I will go to Odysseus's palace and talk to his son, young Telemachus. I must make him ready for his father's return.'

Athene put on her shoes of gold, which carried her as fast as the wind down from Mount Olympus, over land and sea, to the island of Ithaca. As she arrived at Odysseus's palace, she **disguise**d herself as a man called Mentes, a family friend of Odysseus.

Outside the house she found a group of men playing a noisy game while servants were busy around them. Some of the servants were mixing wine and water in bowls; others were piling meat onto plates and preparing the tables for dinner. Odysseus's son, Telemachus, was sitting unhappily among the men, dreaming of his father's return.

Telemachus saw Athene in her disguise, and felt ashamed that no one was greeting the visitor. He hurried towards her. 'Welcome, friend!' he said. 'Come and have some food. Then you can tell us why you are here.'

He led Athene to a table away from the other men, worried that his visitor would be upset by their noise and rudeness. A servant poured water into a fine silver bowl so they could wash their hands. Then plates of bread and meat were brought, and their gold cups were filled with wine.

The other men also ate well, then called for a song from the **bard** Phemius. As Phemius began, Telemachus said to his guest, 'Those men over there worry about nothing except music. They have an easy life, living free while another man pays! If Odysseus returned now, they would wish for a faster pair of legs, not gold or fine clothes. But unfortunately that will never happen. My father was once the

---

fate /feɪt/ (n) the things that happen to someone, especially the unpleasant things
disguise /dɪsˈɡaɪz/ (v, n) to change your appearance so you look like someone else
bard /bɑːd/ (n) a man who sings poems that tell stories of heroes and gods

king of this island, but now his bones are probably being washed by the rain in a faraway land, or by the salt sea waves. No one can give us any news of him. But tell me, what is your name, and what is the reason for your visit?'

'My name is Mentes,' answered bright-eyed Athene. 'My family and yours have been friends for many years. I am here because I heard that your father had already arrived home. The gods must be making his journey difficult, but I am sure that he is still alive. He is a **resourceful** man; he will think of a way to get home. But are you really Odysseus's son? You have grown so tall! You certainly have your father's eyes – although I have not seen him for twenty years, since he left to fight in the Trojan War.'

'Sometimes I wish I had a different father, who was growing old in his own home,' Telemachus replied. 'Odysseus is the most unfortunate man that has ever lived.'

'He is lucky, at least, in his choice of wife, the loving Penelope. But tell me, what are you celebrating with this special meal? And who are these men, who bring no food but behave like the owners of the house? I have never seen such impolite guests.'

'My friend,' Telemachus replied, 'these men have a meal like this every day of the year. My father's disappearance has brought disaster to this house. Many great

resourceful /rɪˈzɔːsfəl/ (adj) good at finding ways to solve problems

2

heroes died in the Trojan War, but their sons are lucky. *Their* fathers left them a famous name. Odysseus was still alive at the end of the war, but he has left me only tears. These men have come from Ithaca and neighbouring lands, hoping to marry my mother. She does not want to accept any of her **suitor**s. But with no news of my father, she cannot refuse them all. They wait for her answer, eating and drinking until we are nearly ruined.'

'How terrible!' the goddess replied. 'They will die if your father ever finds them here. But while he is away, you must try to change the situation yourself. Here is my advice. Choose your best ship, hire a **crew** of twenty strong **oar**smen, and go in search of news of your father. Someone may be able to tell you about him. Go to Pylos first and question its king, wise Nestor. Then continue to King Menelaus in Sparta, since he was the last of the Greeks to reach home. If you hear that your father is alive, prepare yourself for another year with the suitors. But if you hear that he is dead, give your mother in marriage to another man and end the suitors' stay in your house. You are not a child now. Act like a man, and your grandchildren's grandchildren will celebrate your name. But it is getting late. I must return to my ship or my crew will start to worry. Think about my advice.'

'Thank you, good Mentes,' Telemachus said warmly. 'You have shown me the kindness of a father to his son. But will you not stay a little longer? Have a bath and relax. Then you can go back to your ship with a gift from my house – something beautiful and valuable, as you have proved to be a good friend.'

'No,' replied Athene. 'I am in a hurry to get back to my ship and reach my destination, the port of Temesa. But I will be glad to accept a gift on my way home.'

When she had finished speaking, the goddess disappeared suddenly, like a bird through a hole in the roof. Telemachus was left feeling braver and more resourceful than before. Noticing this change, he realised that a god had been with him.

His mind was filled with thoughts of his father as he rejoined the suitors. He found them listening in silence to Phemius, who was singing about the Greeks' problems on their return from the Trojan War.

In her rooms upstairs, Penelope could hear the bard too. She came down the stairs with tears in her eyes.

'Phemius,' she said, 'you know so many wonderful songs about great heroes and powerful gods. Choose one of those songs for tonight, and let the men here drink their wine in peace. But give us no more of your present song. It always

---

suitor /'suːtə, 'sjuː-/ (n) a man who wants to marry a woman; he is her *suitor*
crew /kruː/ (n) the people who work on a ship
oar /ɔː/ (n) a long stick with a wide, flat end, used to pull a boat through water

makes me cry. In the events of your story, no one lost a dearer or a better husband than I, whose husband is famous in every corner of Greece.'

But wise young Telemachus interrupted Penelope. 'Mother,' he said, 'do not stop our great bard from entertaining us as he chooses. The gods are responsible for our fates, not the songs of a bard. It is not surprising that Phemius has chosen this story, as the newest songs are always the most popular. Go back to your rooms, Mother, and busy yourself with your work. I am the **master** of this house, so leave decisions about the entertainment here to me.'

Penelope was surprised by her son's words, but she knew that he spoke wisely. She returned to her rooms, and there she lay crying for Odysseus until the goddess Athene closed her eyes in sleep.

Back in the hall, the suitors were shouting and joking about their hopes to marry the beautiful lady of the house. Telemachus stood up and spoke to them. 'Gentlemen,' he said, 'this is not the way for suitors to behave. Stop this rudeness! Let us enjoy the food and the song – Phemius has the voice of a god. But tomorrow morning there is going to be a meeting. I am going to make a formal request that you leave my house. After tonight, eat your meals somewhere else. If you prefer to destroy my property, then stay. But I will ask Zeus for a day of judgement, and on that day *I* will destroy *you*.'

The suitors were shocked by Telemachus's new confidence. For a moment they did not know what to say. Then Antinous spoke. 'Are the gods teaching you this **arrogance**, Telemachus? If you are already so arrogant now, I hope you never become king of Ithaca.'

master /ˈmɑːstə/ (n) a man who is in charge of other people, especially servants
arrogance /ˈærəɡəns/ (n) behaviour of someone who feels better and more important than other people

'I will gladly become king if the gods wish it,' replied Telemachus. 'But many other princes in Greece want that title and they are welcome to it, since my father is dead. I just want to be the master of my own house, and of the servants won by my father in war.'

Eurymachus now spoke. 'You are right, Telemachus. The gods must decide who Ithaca's next king will be. And you should keep your own property and rule your own house. But tell us, who was your guest and where was he from? Did he bring news of your father, or was he here on business of his own? He left so quickly that we had no opportunity to meet him.'

'There is never any news of my father. We must accept that he is not coming back. My guest was Mentes, an old friend of my father.' Telemachus did not tell them what he knew in his heart – that Mentes was a god in disguise.

The rest of the evening was spent dancing and listening to music. When it grew dark, the suitors slowly returned to their own homes. In his bedroom, Telemachus lay awake all night, thinking about Athene's advice.

The next morning, he called the people of Ithaca to a meeting. When everyone was ready, Telemachus walked to the meeting-place with only two dogs as **companion**s. He looked so proud and confident that everyone's eyes turned to him in admiration. The older men moved away so that he could take his father's seat.

Telemachus stood to address the people. 'I called this meeting, gentlemen, to ask for your help. Great trouble has fallen on my house. First, I have lost my father, Odysseus. But worse than this, a second problem will soon ruin me. A group of suitors spend their days in our house, eating our animals and drinking our wine. Soon all our property will be wasted. Some of the suitors are from the families of Ithaca – some are even here, among us now. Tell them to leave my mother alone. Or did you dislike my father Odysseus's treatment of you, and think that our house deserves these troubles? I would gladly fight all the suitors if I had the strength. But I am one and they are many. I cannot defend our house alone.'

As he spoke, his anger grew, and at the end of his speech his eyes were wet with tears. Many people felt sorry for Telemachus. No one spoke – until Antinous broke the silence.

'What a speech, Telemachus!' he said. 'And what anger! You blame me and the other suitors for your troubles, but you are wrong. The fault is not ours, but your own mother's. For nearly four years she has made us wait for her answer. She gives each of us a reason to hope for her hand in marriage. She makes promises in private messages, but she never keeps those promises. And then there was that **shroud**. "I need to finished it before I marry again," she told us.

---

companion /kəmˈpænjən/ (n) someone that you spend time with or travel with
shroud /ʃraʊd/ (n) a cloth that is put over a dead person's body

"It is to cover the body of Odysseus's father, Laertes, when he dies. It would be bad for my **reputation** if such a great lord had no shroud on his death." We decided to be patient and agree to her wishes. She worked on the shroud every day, but at night she undid all her work. For three years she tricked us in this way. In the end, one of her servants told us of her dishonesty, and we forced her to complete the shroud. But still she has not chosen a husband. This is the suitors' answer, Telemachus. Tell your mother to stop her tricks. We will not leave your house in peace until she has made her choice and married one of us.'

'I cannot force her to marry while she still hopes for my father's return,' replied Telemachus. 'If I did that, the anger of the gods would bring me even more disasters. Go and eat your meals somewhere else. If you stay, the gods will surely punish you for your unlawful behaviour.'

The great god Zeus was listening to his words and sent two **eagle**s to fly above the meeting-place. In the sky, the birds attacked each other, biting each other's faces and necks before flying away over the town. The people stared at the birds, asking themselves what this sign from the gods meant.

Halitherses, a wise old man skilled in **prophecy**, spoke first. 'People of Ithaca, and suitors too, hear my words. Odysseus will not be absent much longer, and his return will bring a violent end to the lives of these arrogant suitors. This will be a disaster for many of us on Ithaca. We must stop the suitors before it is too late. Or even better, the suitors should stop their bad behaviour themselves.'

The suitor Eurymachus stood to reply. 'Go home, old man,' he laughed. 'Tell your stories to your children and leave *us* to understand the signs of the gods. But now *I* will make a prophecy. If you say anything more about Odysseus's return or disaster for the suitors, you yourself will meet a violent end. And this is my advice to Telemachus: he should order his mother to choose a husband. Until she does this, the suitors will never leave. We are afraid of no one – and certainly not of Telemachus and his brave words.'

reputation /ˌrepjʊ'teɪʃən/ (n) the opinion that people have about someone
eagle /'iːgəl/ (n) a very large, strong bird that eats mice and smaller birds
prophecy /'prɒfəsi/ (n) a description of what will happen in the future, usually by a *prophet* who has magical powers

Mentor, an old friend of Odysseus, spoke now. 'People of Ithaca, do you care nothing for Odysseus, who ruled you with the love of a father? Why should a king aim to be fair and kind to his people, if this is your repayment? The suitors are few and you are many. But you sit here in silence and say nothing to criticise their shocking behaviour.'

The suitors shouted over Mentor's words, but Telemachus silenced them. 'Eurymachus and you other suitors,' he said, 'I will say no more. The gods and the people of Ithaca have heard my request. But now, I need a fast ship and a crew of twenty strong men. I am going to Pylos and Sparta to ask for news of my father. If I hear that he is alive, I will wait one more year. But if I hear that he is dead, I will give my mother in marriage to a new husband.'

The suitors laughed at his plan, saying that he would never even find a crew. And so the meeting ended.

Telemachus went to the seashore to think. Athene came to him there, this time disguised as his father's Ithacan friend Mentor. 'Do not worry about the suitors,' she said. 'They are fools. The resourceful son of a resourceful father has nothing to fear from them. I myself will be your companion on your journey. Go back to your house and get food and wine, while I find you a ship and a crew.'

Telemachus returned to his house, where he found the suitors preparing for another great dinner. With a laugh, Antinous ran up to him. 'Come and eat with us,' he called. 'And later I will help you find a ship for your journey.'

'I will make my own arrangements for a ship – and for a nasty end for you suitors too,' replied Telemachus.

Hearing this, all the suitors started shouting. 'He is planning to bring back an army from Pylos to cut our throats!' laughed one.

'Perhaps he will buy some poison to put in our wine-bowl!' cried another.

'Or he may get lost at sea like his father. Oh, how sad that would be! We would have so much trouble sharing his property between us all!' added a third.

Telemachus let them talk. He went downstairs and unlocked a room full of his father's **treasure**. There were piles of gold and silver, clothes, and jars of oil and wine. Everything was being kept safe for Odysseus's return by his loyal servant Eurycleia. Odysseus's father, Laertes, had bought Eurycleia when she was still a girl, for the price of twenty cows. She had looked after both Odysseus and Telemachus when they were babies, and no one loved them more than she did.

Calling the old woman now to the room, Telemachus said, 'Please could you get twelve jars of fine wine for me, and plenty of food? But do not tell anyone! I will come and collect it this evening, when my mother has gone upstairs for the night. I am going to Pylos and Sparta to ask for news of my father.'

There were tears in Eurycleia's eyes as she replied, 'Dear child, no! The suitors will find a way to murder you on your journey and share all this wealth between them. Stay here, at home with your mother, where you belong. Do not go looking for trouble on the stormy seas.'

'Please do not worry, Eurycleia,' answered Telemachus. 'I have the gods on my side. But promise me that you will not tell my mother that I have gone. We do not want to upset her for no reason.'

Eurycleia promised to keep his secret and started organising the food and drink. Telemachus went back upstairs to the hall and rejoined the suitors.

At the same time, Athene was going round the town disguised as Telemachus, choosing twenty strong men for the ship's crew. She had already borrowed a ship from an Ithacan man called Noemon. When the ship and crew were ready, she returned to Odysseus's palace and made the suitors sleepy. They soon found that they could not keep their eyes open, so one after the other they went to bed.

Athene took on the appearance of Mentor again, and went to find Telemachus. 'Come,' she said to him. 'Twenty companions are sitting at their oars, waiting to start their journey. Let us not delay.'

Telemachus followed Athene to the ship. The food and wine was carried on board, and soon they were at sea. Athene called for a good wind to take them to Pylos, and Telemachus ordered his men to put up the sail. As night turned to day, the ship was making good progress on its way to Pylos.

---

treasure /'treʒə/ (n) gold, silver, jewels and other valuable things

CHAPTER 2

Telemachus's Travels

*'If Odysseus ever proved that he was your friend in the hard years of the war,
tell me everything that you know about his death.'*

A s Telemachus and his companions came near to Pylos, they saw a great crowd of people on the beach, including King Nestor and his family. Telemachus's crew brought the ship to land. Then they all followed Athene, who was still disguised as Mentor, onto the shore.

Telemachus was the last to leave the ship. As they walked towards the crowd, Athene said to him, 'Remember, this is not a time to be shy. We are here to find out how your father's life ended. Go, then, and ask Nestor confidently if he has any news.'

'But I will be embarrassed, talking in public to Nestor,' Telemachus replied. 'He is so much older than me and so famous. I have no experience of public life. How should I speak to him?'

'Do not worry,' Athene advised. 'When your own words fail you, the gods will help. They are looking kindly on this journey of yours.'

When they reached the crowd, they were greeted warmly by Nestor and his family, who had just made a **sacrifice** to the sea-god Poseidon. The king's son, Peisistratus, offered them some meat from the sacrificed cows, and servants poured them some wine. After they had finished the wonderful food, Nestor

sacrifice /ˈsækrəfaɪs/ (n, v) the killing of an animal as a gift to a god

spoke. 'Who are you, friends, and where have you come from? What is your business here in Pylos?'

Athene gave Telemachus the confidence to reply. 'Nestor, son of Neleus, great hero of the Greeks, we are from the island of Ithaca. I have come here looking for news of my father, long-suffering Odysseus. It is said that he fought by your side until the end of the Trojan War. But he has never come home, and no one can tell us when or where he died.'

'Ah, my friend,' cried King Nestor, 'what memories I have of that long war! It would take years just to tell you of all the disasters that struck us at Troy. We lost our best men there – Achilles, Patroclus, and my own son Antilochus too, a handsome boy, fast and strong.

'For nine years we tried to beat the Trojans, but Zeus threw many difficulties in our path. In all those years, no one showed better judgement than Odysseus – your father, if you really are his son. It is not hard to believe, since you look and speak exactly like him. In all those long years, your wise father and I never once spoke on opposite sides of an argument. At every stage of the war, we agreed on the best plan of action.

'After we destroyed the city of Troy, we left in our ships. But then Zeus sent us all in different directions, because some people among us had displeased the gods. We had arguments about the route home, and some ships were caught by storms. I myself was lucky – my voyage was very smooth. So I heard no news of the other commanders.

'But what is the news from Ithaca? Are the stories true, that a crowd of your mother's suitors are living as uninvited guests in your house? I only wish that the goddess Athene showed you some of the kindness that helped your father so much during the war. If she cared for *you* like that, the suitors would soon have their thoughts of marriage knocked out of them.'

'Good Nestor,' replied Telemachus, 'I cannot hope for an end to my troubles with the suitors, even if it is the gods' dearest wish.'

'Telemachus,' interrupted bright-eyed Athene, 'what are you saying? Nothing is impossible if the gods are helping you.'

'The gods have already sent my father to his death, Mentor,' said Telemachus to the goddess. 'Is that their way of helping my family?'

'Well, my advice to you, Telemachus,' continued Nestor, 'is to go home quickly and guard your property from the greedy suitors. But there is one more person that you should visit. Menelaus has only just returned home, after years lost at sea. Perhaps he will have news of your father. Go now, with your ship and crew; or my sons can go with you by land, and show you the way to red-haired Menelaus's palace in Sparta.'

Darkness was falling, so Nestor invited them to stay the night at the palace.

'You are very kind, my lord,' said Athene. 'Telemachus will gladly accept your invitation, but I must return to the ship. In the morning the crew and I must continue our voyage. Telemachus can travel to Sparta in one of your **chariot**s, if your son can be his companion.'

When she finished, the goddess turned into a bird and flew away. Nestor and Telemachus stared at the sky in shock. 'Telemachus, my boy!' cried Nestor, 'I think your friend Mentor was really Athene, whose help was so valuable to your father. With a goddess at your side, you have a great future ahead of you!'

Telemachus spent the night in Nestor's palace, and in the morning Nestor's son Peisistratus called for a chariot to take them to Sparta.

They arrived two days later and found Menelaus celebrating a family wedding. A bard and dancers were entertaining the guests in the hall as they ate their dinner.

Telemachus and Peisistratus stopped their chariot outside the palace. Menelaus's friend Eteoneus came out of the hall and saw them there. He hurried to his king, saying, 'There are two strangers at the gates. Should we welcome them inside or ask them to continue on their journey?'

chariot /'tʃæriət/ (n) a vehicle with two wheels, pulled by a horse

11

Red-haired Menelaus answered him angrily. 'Eteoneus, you are not usually a fool, but you are certainly talking like one now. You and I enjoyed the welcome of strangers in many far lands before we reached home. Go and help our guests at once, and invite them to join us.'

Telemachus and Peisistratus were soon following Eteoneus into the palace, where they were washed by the servant-girls and dressed in fine new clothes. Then they took their seats next to Menelaus in the hall.

The servants brought them food and drink and Menelaus greeted them warmly. Telemachus whispered to Peisistratus, 'Look at this room! Have you ever seen so much gold? Surely even Zeus's palace on Mount Olympus does not shine as brightly!'

Menelaus heard his words and said, 'No one's home can compare with the palace of the gods, dear boy. But few ordinary men have collected more treasure than I have. For seven long years I travelled the world and made my fortune – in Cyprus, Egypt, Ethiopia and Libya. But there were many hard times during those years, and while I was away, my brother was cruelly murdered by his wife and her lover. I would happily exchange all the gold and silver in this house for the return of my brother and the friends who I lost at Troy.

'But although I miss every one of my lost companions, there is one whose death upsets me even more than the rest. Odysseus always tried harder, fought harder, thought harder than anyone else in the war. But his resourcefulness did not help him in the end. He has never returned home. I often think of his family – his father, old Laertes, his loyal wife, Penelope, and his son Telemachus, who was only a baby when Odysseus left for the war. It must be hard to wait for him year after year. They have probably given up waiting now. It is twenty years since he was last in Ithaca.'

These words brought tears to Telemachus's eyes, and Menelaus realised at once who his young visitor must be. As he was deciding what to say to him, his wife Helen arrived in the hall. Everyone's eyes followed her across the room in admiration. Long ago, her beauty had been the cause of the Trojan War. A Trojan prince, Paris, had stolen her from her husband's home in Sparta and taken her to live with him in Troy. The Greeks had attacked the Trojans to win her back. Now, returned to her loving husband, her goddess-like beauty still shone bright.

One of her ladies helped her into a chair; another brought her a fine blanket of the softest wool; a third passed her her silver work-basket, a gift from a friend in Egypt. As Helen started her work, she asked her husband about the visitors. 'Do we know their names, Menelaus? I must say, that young man looks exactly like Odysseus. Could he be Odysseus's son, who was only a baby when the Greek army followed me to Troy?'

'I think you are right,' her husband replied. 'A few minutes ago he was crying when I spoke of my memories of Odysseus.'

Peisistratus now spoke. 'Menelaus, great king, you have guessed rightly. My friend here is Odysseus's son, Telemachus, and I am Peisistratus, son of Nestor. Because Telemachus is shy in the company of great men like yourself, my father asked me to be his companion here.'

'Well, he is a very welcome visitor,' cried Menelaus. 'I had hoped to build his father a home near mine, so that we could meet regularly and continue to be friends. But a jealous god has robbed me of this happy future.'

Everyone's eyes filled with tears. For some time they were silent, lost in their own unhappy thoughts, until Peisistratus said, 'The dead deserve our tears, but this is meant to be a wedding celebration. Let us talk of happier subjects.'

'Wise words, Peisistratus,' replied Menelaus. 'You have your father's good sense.' He called for more food and wine, and their good humour slowly returned.

After a comfortable night in the palace, Telemachus was woken by Menelaus. 'What is the purpose of your visit here, Telemachus?' he asked. 'Is it public business or a private matter?'

'Great king, I came here to ask you for news of my father. My mother is surrounded by arrogant suitors, who spend their days as uninvited guests in my house. They will not leave until my mother chooses one of them, but she delays her choice as she is still hoping for my father's return. So the suitors wait in my hall, eating my meat and drinking my wine until I am nearly ruined. I have come here to ask if you have any information about my father. Please, if Odysseus ever proved that he was your friend in the hard years of the war, tell me everything that you know about his death.'

'I cannot believe that those cowardly suitors are planning to take brave Odysseus's place in Ithaca! Ha! They will get a shock if Odysseus ever returns – and a quick death too. But to answer your question, I will tell you everything I heard from the god Proteus, whose lips can never lie.

'I was in Egypt. For twenty days my companions and I had been on an island in the mouth of the Nile with no wind to take our ships home. We had no more food and were starting to fear for our lives. But luckily the goddess Eidothee, Proteus's daughter, saw us there and felt sorry for us. "My father, sea-loving Proteus, lives on this island," she said. "He can tell you how to get home. He can also tell you what has happened in Greece while you have been away."

'"But how will I make your father tell me all this?" I asked her. "Proteus does not give information willingly."

'"When the sun is high in the sky, Proteus comes out of the sea and sleeps on the beach with the **seal**s. If you and a few companions dress in seal skins, you can hide on the beach and surprise him. Hold him down with all your strength. He will turn into all kinds of shapes as he tries to escape you. But if this fails, he will finally change back to his normal shape. Then you can let him go, and he will answer all your questions."

'The next day we did as Eidothee suggested. At sunrise, she dug holes in the sand. We climbed inside and she put seal skins over our bodies. There we waited, with the horrible smell of dead seals in our noses. Soon a great crowd of seals came out of the sea and lay down around us on the beach, and at midday Proteus joined them for a sleep. With a shout, we jumped on him and held him tightly. Immediately he started turning into different kinds of animal, then into water and into a tree, but he could not escape us. Finally he changed back into his normal shape, and I said to him, "Are you going to change shape all day, or will you tell us what we need to know? We have been unable to leave this island for twenty days. What can we do to get home?"

'"You did not sacrifice to the gods before you started your voyage," Proteus said, "so now they are angry with you. If you want to see your home again, you will have to sail the waters of the Nile once more and make the right sacrifices. Then your voyage home can continue."

seal /siːl/ (n) a large sea animal that eats fish and can move slowly on land

'My heart was filled with sadness at the thought of returning to the Egyptian mainland. But I hid my feelings and said, "I will do as you say. But tell me, what news is there of the rest of the Greek army? Has everyone reached home safely?"

'"Why, Menelaus, are you asking me this? I warn you, you will cry an ocean of tears when you hear my answer. Most of the Greek commanders are now safe in their homes, but two have died. A third, though alive, is held prisoner on an unknown island, far from his friends and loving family.

'"Ajax was the first to die, in a terrible storm at Gyrae. But your brother Agamemnon, who had been with Ajax just before the storm, was lucky and sailed from Gyrae with all his ships unharmed. It seemed that he had escaped his fate. When he landed safely in his homeland, Mycenae, he kissed the earth in happiness. His arrival, though, was watched by one of Aegisthus's spies.

'"While you and your brother were at Troy, your cousin Aegisthus had turned his attention to wife-stealing. Your brother's wife, Clytemnestra, was his prize. At first she had listened to his words of love with deaf ears, but before long she had become his willing lover. Now Aegisthus was waiting for Agamemnon's return. He had already won the wife. Next he was planning to murder the husband and rule the great lands of Mycenae in his place.

'"When Aegisthus heard the spy's news, he sent soldiers to hide in Agamemnon's palace. Then he went in his chariot to meet the king. Your brother, never guessing Aegisthus's terrible plans, came up with him from the coast and they celebrated his return together. Then Aegisthus killed him in his own palace, as a man might sacrifice a cow to the gods. Agamemnon's companions were murdered too. There was not a single man left alive."

'This was Proteus's story, and it broke my heart. I sat down on the sands and cried. After some time, Proteus interrupted me, saying, "You have cried long enough! Waste no more time in tears. Is it not better to do everything in your power to reach home, so that you can punish Aegisthus for his crime?"

'These words made me feel a little better. "You have described the fates of two Greek commanders. Who is the third, who is a prisoner on an unknown island? Please tell me his name, even if it brings me more unhappiness."

'"The third is Odysseus," he replied. "I saw him on the island of the goddess Calypso, with tears running down his face. His only desire is to return to Ithaca, but Calypso is in love with him and does not want him to leave. Without her help, he is a prisoner on the island – he has no ship or crew to carry him home."

'The old man had nothing more to say. Soon he sank back into the deep salt waters, and I returned with my companions to the ships. The next day, we sailed back to the Egyptian mainland, and there we made the right sacrifices to the gods. We also built a great **mound** of earth, so that the name of Agamemnon would live in that far land for ever.

'From that moment, our voyage home was easy. I was only sorry that I returned too late to punish Aegisthus for his terrible crime. Agamemnon's son, my nephew Orestes, had already killed that murderer and sent him to the fate that the gods had chosen for him.

'But now, my friend, please stay in my palace for as long as you can. And you must take some gifts home with you – three horses, perhaps, and a fine chariot.'

'I would love to stay longer, Menelaus,' Telemachus answered, 'but my friends in Pylos are waiting for me. And though horses are a generous gift, I cannot take them. Ithaca is a rocky land, with no fields for horses to run. They will be more useful here in Sparta.'

'Then I will find you another gift,' smiled Menelaus. 'I will give you the most valuable and beautiful treasure that my palace holds – a silver mixing bowl edged with gold. It was a gift to me from the King of Sidon.'

◆

In front of Odysseus's palace, the suitors were sitting and joking as usual. Noemon came to Antinous and handsome Eurymachus. 'Do you know when Telemachus is expected home from Pylos? He went in my ship, and I need it for a voyage to my farm on Elis.'

---

mound /maʊnd/ (n) a pile of earth or stones that looks like a small hill

'Pylos!' cried Antinous. 'I thought he was up in the hills of Ithaca with his pigs and his sheep.'

'Yes, we all thought that,' agreed Eurymachus. 'Noemon, tell us exactly what you know.'

'He left several days ago, and his crew were the best young men on Ithaca, after ourselves. Mentor went as his captain – well, it looked like Mentor on the ship, but in fact I saw Mentor here on Ithaca yesterday. Very strange!'

As Noemon walked away, Antinous and Eurymachus called all the suitors together.

'Telemachus is in trouble now,' thundered Antinous. 'We said that his voyage to Pylos would never happen. And he has already gone, taking the best men on Ithaca with him! There is only one way to answer this arrogance. Give me a fast ship and a strong crew, and I will wait for him in the water between Ithaca and the Samian rocks. His voyage to find his father is going to end in blood.'

The other suitors agreed to this plan, and asked Antinous to make all the arrangements.

The servant Medon heard their conversation and ran to tell his queen. When Penelope heard the news, her knees shook and her eyes filled with tears. 'But why has my son gone?' she asked Medon. 'Does he want his bones to join his father's, washed by the salt sea waves?'

'I understand that he was looking for news of his father, my lady,' replied Medon, leaving the room quietly.

Penelope fell to the floor. Her women-servants surrounded her as she cried, 'Is there any woman whose fate is crueller than mine? Zeus gave me a good husband, then took him from me. And now my son has been stolen away without a word. And you servants are cruel too. You all knew of Telemachus's voyage, I am sure. Why did no one wake me from my bed as he went to his ship, so that I could stop this foolish adventure?'

'Dear lady,' replied old Eurycleia, 'I knew all about his voyage, and I even gave him the food that he needed for it. But he made me promise that I would not tell you. He did not want to upset you unnecessarily. Now, go and wash, and put on some fresh clothes. Then **pray** to Athene. Although the danger is great, the goddess may be able to save him.'

While Penelope prayed to Athene, Antinous and his crew prepared their ship. As the sky grew dark, they left the shore and sailed to Asteris, a little island between Ithaca and the rocky coast of Samos. There they waited for Telemachus's ship to come into view.

pray /preɪ/ (v) to speak to a god, usually to ask for something or to give thanks

2.1 Were you right?

Look at your answers to Activity 1.2 on page iv. Then complete these sentences.

1 Telemachus is Odysseus's .... He .... Odysseus
   to return, but he is .... with him.

2 Penelope is Odysseus's .... She .... Odysseus.

3 Eurymachus is one of the .... He .... Odysseus
   to return.

4 Eurycleia is Odysseus's .... She .... Odysseus.

2.2 What more did you learn?

Complete this text.

Menelaus, King of (1)_____,
has returned from the war in
(2)_____ with his wife (3)_____.
He visited many places on his way
home, including the River (4)_____.
He is very upset about the murder of his
brother, (5)_____, by his cousin,
(6)_____, but is pleased that his
cousin has been punished for
the crime.

2.3 Language in use

**Look at the sentences on the right.
Then rewrite these sentences using
passive verb forms.**

Everything **was being kept** safe for
Odysseus's return.

'And now my son **has been stolen** away.'

1 The gods are helping Odysseus.
   Odysseus is being helped by the gods.

2 The people of Ithaca have not seen Odysseus for twenty years.
   Odysseus ....
   ....

3 Has a storm destroyed Odysseus's ships?
   Have Odysseus's ships ....
   ....

4 The Greeks and Trojans were fighting a long war.
   A long war ....
   ....

5 Helen had caused the Greeks' attack on Troy.
   The Greeks' attack ....
   ....

2.4 What happens next?

Look at this picture. Match the questions with the answers.

1 Who is in the picture?   **a** Princess Nausicaa

2 Who tells him to make this journey?   **b** Odysseus

3 Who starts the storm?   **c** the sea-god Poseidon

4 Who helps the man after he escapes the storm?   **d** Calypso

CHAPTER 3

Leaving Calypso

'Even well-built ships do not cross this endless sea. It would be mad to travel such a long distance in a home-made raft.'

While Athene was helping young Telemachus, Zeus sent his messenger Hermes to talk to the goddess Calypso. For many years, Odysseus had been an unwilling guest on Calypso's island.

Outside Calypso's **cave**, Hermes stopped to admire the beautiful scene. A little stream ran between trees filled with birdsong, and flowers and fruit grew everywhere. A fire burned brightly at the cave's entrance, and inside he could hear Calypso singing.

When she noticed the god entering her home, she said, 'Hermes, you are welcome. Come and have something to eat, and tell me what brings you here.'

'I have been sent here by Zeus,' he replied. 'I had no wish to make this long journey – across endless, empty sea, with no cities or people on the way. But no one can refuse the orders of Zeus. This is Zeus's message: it is not Odysseus's fate to end his days on your island, so send him on his way without delay. He must continue his voyage to Ithaca.'

Calypso's body shook with sadness. 'Zeus is so unfair. He himself is allowed any number of human girlfriends. But if a goddess finds love with a human, he ends her happiness immediately. I saved Odysseus from death after his ship was destroyed in a storm; I welcomed him here on my island and looked after all his needs; I even offered to turn him into a god. But now Zeus orders me to let him go. Well, I must do it – I have no choice. But I have no boat to give him, and the voyage is long. I can only tell him the direction to take.'

'Then send him on his way at once and you will not have to worry about Zeus's anger.' With these words, Hermes started his journey back to the palace of the gods.

Calypso went at once to look for Odysseus. She found him sitting on the shore, crying for his lost home as usual. 'Dry your tears,' she said to him, 'and waste no more of your life on this island that brings you no pleasure. I am ready to help you leave. Cut down some trees and make a **raft**. I will give you food and drink for your voyage. I will even give you a wind that will blow you to Ithaca, if more powerful gods do not stop me.'

'Even well-built ships do not cross this endless sea,' he replied. 'It would be mad to travel such a long distance in a home-made raft. I will not do it. Or can you give me your word that this is not a trick to cause me more trouble?'

---

cave /keɪv/ (n) a large, natural hole in a rock wall or under the ground
raft /rɑːft/ (n) pieces of wood tied together into a platform that is used like a boat

Calypso smiled and touched his face with her hand. 'How can you think that I would trick you like that? By the earth and the sky and by death itself, I promise you: I am just trying to help.'

After they had eaten together in the cave, she said, 'So have you definitely decided to leave? Please think again. I know you miss your wife Penelope, but you will have so much pain and suffering before you reach your homeland. Is it not better to stay here with me? A goddess is more beautiful than any human wife, and with me you can escape death forever by becoming a god.'

'Do not be angry with me, goddess,' he replied. 'Of course you are more beautiful than Penelope, but I want nothing more than to return home to my family. And I stopped worrying about the dangers of my journey long ago. I have suffered so much already. One more disaster means nothing to me now.'

When morning came, Calypso gave Odysseus some tools and he started work on his raft. After four days of hard work, the raft was ready. It had a cloth sail, and plenty of food and drink on board. A warm and gentle wind blew up at Calypso's command, and with a happy heart Odysseus sailed out to sea.

Keeping his eyes on the stars, he travelled east for seventeen days without sleeping, and on the eighteenth day the land of the Phaeacians came into view. But Poseidon, god of the sea, saw Odysseus on his raft and the sight made him angry. 'It seems that the other gods have changed their minds about Odysseus,' he said to himself. 'He has nearly reached the land of the Phaeacians, where his suffering is going to end. But I have not forgiven him for the harm he did to my son. It is not too late to send a little more trouble in his direction.'

With those words, he covered both land and sea with thick fog. Then he called all the winds together to make a violent storm, and enormous waves crashed down on Odysseus's raft.

'Oh gods!' cried Odysseus, 'have you not finished with me yet? Calypso's prophecy is coming true – that I will have more pain and suffering before I reach my homeland. How lucky were my companions who were killed at Troy! They died with their friends around them, and their names live forever; I am going to die in a sea storm, alone and forgotten.'

As he spoke, a wave the size of a mountain thundered down on him and threw him off the raft. The waters closed over his head. His clothes – a gift from Calypso – were heavy in the water, and made swimming difficult. But at last he reached the air and coughed out the salt water from his mouth. With the last of his energy, he swam back to the raft and threw himself on board. He held on tightly, but the violent winds drove him in every direction except to safety.

Then Poseidon sent another enormous wave towards him. For a second or two, it hung above his head, then it crashed violently down on the raft, throwing the wood in all directions. Odysseus held onto a piece of wood, kicked off his clothes and bravely started swimming.

Poseidon laughed when he saw this. 'It is a long way to the coast, Odysseus, but swim there if you can. I have had my fun with you.'

Athene now sent the south, east and west winds back to bed. She calmed the north wind so it could blow Odysseus gently towards the land of the Phaeacians. For two days and two nights he swam. Time after time he thought he would die, but on the third day, a wave lifted him a little and he saw that land was near. He felt like a child who learns that his father, after suffering from a long and painful illness, has been cured. Odysseus felt a similar happiness when he saw the welcome sight of hills and trees. He swam more quickly in his excitement, until he heard the thunder of the waves on the rocks ahead. Too late, he realised that there were no beaches to land on; there were only sharp walls of broken rock. An enormous wave lifted him towards them, and it looked like certain death. But luckily he managed to save himself by catching onto a rock with both hands. The powerful waves soon pulled his hands away, and he was back under water. He kicked hard to reach the air. Finally, he decided to swim further along the shore, although he was already so tired.

At last Odysseus came to a more welcoming coastline. He found the mouth of a stream, and there he landed safely. He fell to the ground, too weak to move. He lay there for some time, until he realised that it was getting late. With no clothes, he might freeze at night if he stayed where he was. But was he safer in the woods, where wild animals might be looking for an easy supper? After some thought, he chose the warmer ground of the woods, and looked for a suitable place to sleep. He found two trees growing together so tightly that their branches kept out the wind and sun and rain. Between these trees he lay down and covered himself with a blanket of dry leaves. For the first time in three weeks, he fell asleep.

◆

As Odysseus slept, Athene went to the palace of Alcinous, the Phaeacian king. Alcinous had a young daughter called Nausicaa, as tall and beautiful as a goddess. Athene, disguised as one of Nauiscaa's friends, went into her bedroom and whispered in her ear as she slept in her soft bed. 'Nausicaa, why are you being so lazy? You will need lots of fine clothes when you are married, but all *your* clothes are lying around the palace unwashed. Let us go and wash them together in the morning. We must hurry. The young men from every good family in the land want to marry you, and your father will certainly choose a husband for you soon.'

Athene then returned to her home on Mount Olympus, and a little later Nausicaa woke up. Remembering the strange dream that she had had in the night, she immediately went to find her father. 'Father, could I have one of the horses today, and a vehicle to carry our dirty clothes to the stream? Your own clothes need washing, and my brothers often ask for clean clothes to wear at their dances.' She did not talk about her own marriage – she was too shy to discuss this matter with her father. But he understood completely and replied, 'The servants will bring you what you need, my child.'

While the servants brought a vehicle and a horse, Nausicaa rushed around the palace collecting her family's finest and most colourful clothes. Her mother packed her some food and wine for the trip, and soon Nausicaa and a group of her friends were on their way to the stream, talking happily.

There were some deep pools in the stream, perfect for washing the clothes. The girls threw them into the water by the armful and started their work. When everything was clean, they stretched out the clothes on the beach. Then they bathed in the stream and sat down for some food while the sunshine dried the clothes.

When they had finished their meal, they started playing a ball game, and Nausicaa sang the instructions. She looked like a young goddess, more beautiful than all the beautiful girls around her.

The girls' voices woke Odysseus and he got out of his bed between the trees to see what was happening. Luckily, he remembered that he was wearing no clothes, and used some leaves to hide his body. But he looked dirty and wild after his terrible days at sea, like a dangerous animal mad with hunger. When the girls saw him, they screamed and ran away. Only Nausicaa stayed to face him.

Odysseus's first thought was to throw his arms around the beautiful girl's knees and ask her for help. But he did not want to upset her by touching her. Instead, he kept his distance and said, 'Are you a human or a goddess? I cannot guess the answer, since I have never seen such beauty. If you have a human family, how lucky they are! What pleasure they must feel when you dance in their company. And luckiest of all is the man who takes you home as his wife.

'Princess, I must ask you for help. Yesterday I arrived on this shore, carried here by the winds after three weeks on the stormy seas. My raft and my clothes are lost, and I know no one in this land. Pity me in my troubles. Tell me, please, how do I reach your city? And do you have anything that I can use for clothes?'

'Sir,' she replied, 'you will be given everything that you need. The king of this land is Alcinous, and I am his daughter. I will gladly show you the way to his palace.'

'I thank you with all my heart,' answered Odysseus.

Nausicaa now called to her friends. 'Come back, girls. There is nothing to fear. This man is an unlucky voyager and we will help him, since all strangers are protected by Zeus.'

Odysseus washed his salty skin in the stream, while the girls looked for some clothes to give him. As he dressed, clean at last, Athene used her powers to make him taller and stronger, with thicker hair. Nausicaa whispered to her friends, 'When I first saw this man, I thought he was terribly unattractive; now, though, he looks more like the gods on Olympus. How I would like a man like this as my husband! Hurry, now, girls. Take him something to eat and drink.'

Odysseus was very grateful for the food. While he ate hungrily, the girls packed up the washed clothes. Then Nausicaa called to Odysseus, 'We are going back to the city now. I am sure you will understand when I ask you to follow with my friends only as far as the city gates. Inside the city, I must be more careful of my reputation. You can imagine what people will say if they see me with a handsome stranger. They will guess that I have refused all the men from local families and chosen a foreign husband instead, or that a god has taken me as his wife. That kind of talk will not help me to find a good husband when the time comes. So, we will leave you at the entrance to the city. Give us time to return to the palace, then join us there later. In the city, look at no one and ask no questions. My people are great sailors, thanks to Poseidon, with the fastest ships in the world – but they are not always good hosts. When you enter the palace, look for my mother, Queen Arete. She usually sits next to my father in the great hall and, as the daughter of the last king, she is as powerful and popular as King Alcinous himself. Throw your arms around her knees and ask for her help. If she feels pity for your situation, you will soon see your homeland again.'

Odysseus willingly agreed to the plan. At the entrance to the city, he waited while the princess and her friends returned to the palace. Athene threw a magic fog over him so that no one could see him as he walked through the city. When he reached the gates of the palace, he was almost blinded by the shining sight that met his eyes. Hanging on silver posts were two great doors of gold, and inside were hundreds of beautiful works of art, also made of gold. Around the palace was a brightly coloured garden full of tall fruit trees.

Still protected by Athene's magic fog, he entered the palace. He found the great hall and walked, unseen, past a long table of Phaeacians eating dinner. When he got to Queen Arete's seat, he threw his arms round her knees and, at the same moment, Athene lifted the fog from his shoulders. Everyone in the room looked at him in shock.

CHAPTER 4

With the Phaeacians

'I can think of no better companion for my daughter. I would give you a house and great treasures if you were willing to stay here as her husband.'

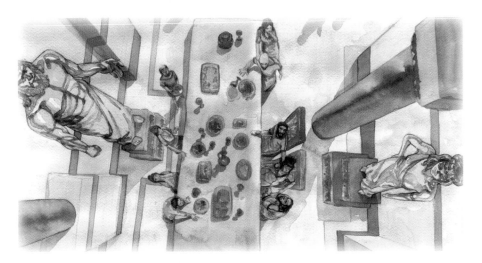

'Arete, great queen,' said Odysseus, 'I am here to ask you and your royal husband for help. I pray that the gods give your family good fortune and great happiness. For myself, my dearest wish is to return to my home across the seas, after all the disasters that I have suffered.'

No one spoke, and Odysseus sat down on the floor by the fire. At last, the silence was broken by an older Phaeacian man named Echeneus. 'My king, it is not right to let this man sit on the floor. Offer him one of our silver chairs to sit on, and ask the servants to bring him some wine. We should pray to Zeus, protector of strangers.'

Alcinous did as Echeneus suggested, giving Odysseus the seat where his favourite son usually sat. When Odysseus had had food and drink, Alcinous said, 'Phaeacians, we have eaten well. Now it is time for you to return to your homes for the night. In the morning, we will decide how to arrange this stranger's safe return to his homeland.'

The Phaeacian guests left the room. While the servants cleared the tables, Arete looked more closely at Odysseus and recognised the clothes that he was wearing. She herself had made them with her ladies' help. 'Sir,' she said, 'who are you? And who gave you those clothes? Did you say that you have come here from across the sea?'

'Great queen, it would be boring for you to listen to all my troubles, as the gods have sent me so many. But I will tell you this. I have come from an island far out to sea, the home of the goddess Calypso. Before that, I was travelling with my companions, but they all died when Zeus destroyed our ship. Only I managed to stay alive, by holding onto a piece of the broken ship until the winds blew me to Calypso's shore. For seven years she tried to win my love, and for all that time I was an unhappy prisoner on her island. But, finally, she allowed me to leave. I made a raft and sailed safely until I caught sight of the mountains here in Phaeacian lands. But then Poseidon sent a storm to destroy my raft, and I nearly lost my life many times as I swam to your shore.

'I slept near the coast, and in the morning I was woken by your daughter and her friends. I asked her for help and she gave me these clothes. You should be proud of her. She has the beauty of a goddess, and the good sense too.'

'She made one mistake,' said Alcinous. 'Why did she not bring you home with her friends?'

'Do not blame your daughter, great king,' replied Odysseus. 'She wanted me to follow her. It was my decision to stay behind, fearing that you would not like a stranger as your daughter's companion.'

'My friend, I can think of no better companion for my daughter. I would give you a house and great treasures if you were willing to stay here as her husband. But we will not keep you here by force. Tomorrow you can make your voyage home. It will only take a day – it does not matter how far you are going. You will soon learn why the Phaeacians have such a good reputation as seamen.'

Odysseus's heart filled with happiness as he heard Alcinous's words. Arete showed him to the bed that the servants had prepared for him, and he spent the night dreaming of a happy return to Ithaca.

In the morning, fifty-two young men were chosen as the crew for the voyage to Odysseus's homeland. They prepared their boat down at the port, then came to the palace for a meal. When they had eaten, Alcinous called for his bard, Demodocus.

'Demodocus, the gods have given you a special gift. Your songs never fail to please our ears, whatever subject you choose for your story. Sing!'

Demodocus sang of the Trojan War, and the argument between Odysseus and Achilles that had started a great wave of disasters for the Greeks. As Odysseus listened to the bard's song, he put his hands over his face and cried. He tried to hide his tears from the Phaeacians, but Alcinous noticed his sadness. Not wishing to upset his guest, he stopped Demodocus after a pause in the song. 'Good people, we have enjoyed the food and the song. Now let us go outside and show our guest that the Phaeacians are also good sportsmen.'

Everyone followed Alcinous to the city's meeting-place. The finest young men in the land rushed forward to show their skill. First there was a running race. A great cloud of dust followed the runners around the course. Euryalus was soon far ahead of the rest, and won the race easily. Next came throwing, jumping and fighting competitions; each had a different winner. Alcinous's son Laodamas, who had won the fighting, then went to Odysseus and said, 'Come, sir, and join our games. Forget your troubles for a few minutes, since you will soon be back in your homeland. If you are good at sport, there is no better way to make a famous name for yourself.'

Odysseus replied, 'My heart is too full of sadness to play in your games. I have suffered disaster after disaster, and now I can think of nothing except my voyage home.'

Euryalus, the winner of the running race, joined them. 'We understand, sir,' he said. 'We were wrong to think that you might have strength or speed. You are more like a sea captain, worrying about his business and his ship. Clearly you are not a sportsman.'

Odysseus gave him an angry look. 'You should be ashamed of yourself for that insult,' he said angrily. 'Some men do not have the fortune of good looks, but they win popularity with the people for their fine intelligence and wise words. Others – and you are one – are good-looking but arrogant, with no good sense at all. Your words have angered me. I am not unskilled at sport, as you suggest, but after years

at war and on the stormy seas I am not as strong as I once was. I will join your competition, though, if you wish it. I will not listen to more of your insults.'

Odysseus jumped from his seat and picked up a stone disk, much bigger than the ones that the Phaeacians usually used. Putting all his weight into the throw, he sent the disk flying through the air. It landed far beyond the throw that had won the competition earlier.

Odysseus turned to the Phaeacians with a smile. 'Now beat that if you can,' he said. 'But I will probably make an even longer throw in a minute. You said that you wanted a competition. Well, I am happy to beat you in a fight, or with a **bow** and **arrow**. I am confident that I can win at anything except running. I am weak after my days at sea, and a younger man would probably be faster on his legs.'

'My friend,' said King Alcinous, 'I do not blame you for your anger. Euryalus was wrong to speak to you as he did. But let us forget the games. When you are at home with your wife and children, I want you to tell them of our special Phaeacian skills. We are not the world's greatest fighters or throwers, but we can run fast and we are excellent seamen. We are also very proud of the fine food, music and dance at our dinners, and of our wonderful hot baths and comfortable beds. So come, forget the games, and let our dancers perform for you. And later our bard Demodocus can entertain us with his songs.'

For the rest of the afternoon, Odysseus watched the traditional dances of the Phaeacians and listened to Demodocus's stories of the gods. The entertainment ended with a dance by two of Alcinous's sons, Laodamas and Halius, in which they threw a purple ball to each other as they moved in time to the music. 'You are right to be proud of your dancers,' Odysseus said to his host. 'I have never seen such a wonderful performance.'

His words pleased Alcinous. 'Phaeacians,' said the king, 'we must give our guest suitable gifts to take home. I and the other twelve princes of the land should each give him some fine clothes and a bar of gold. And Euryalus should add his own gift too, to apologise for his rudeness at the games.'

Everyone agreed with Alcinous's suggestion and the gifts were organised at once. Euryalus gave Odysseus a well-made **sword**, saying, 'Sir, your visit has been a great pleasure to the Phaeacian people. If my words upset you, let the winds blow them away. I pray to the gods that you have a safe voyage on our ship and a warm welcome when you reach your home.'

'Friend,' replied Odysseus, 'I thank you, and pray that the gods give you a happy life. Your words at the games are now forgotten.'

bow /baʊ/ (n) a long, thin, curved piece of wood, with a tight string across it, used to shoot arrows
arrow /'ærəʊ/ (n) a thin stick with a sharp metal end that you shoot with a bow
sword /sɔːd/ (n) a long piece of metal with a handle, which was used in war

Queen Arete packed the new clothes and the gold in a chest, and added a gold cup from her husband. Then the servants poured Odysseus a hot bath – and what a pleasure it was to lie in that bath, after his hard weeks at sea.

When he was dressed, he went back to the great hall. Nausicaa was standing at the entrance to the hall, looking like a goddess. She was filled with admiration when she saw Odysseus. 'Good luck, my friend,' she said. 'Think of me sometimes when you are safely back home. You would not be alive without me.'

'Princess Nausicaa,' replied Odysseus, 'I pray that Zeus will soon let me see my home again. If he does, I will always remember you.'

With these words, he entered the hall and took his seat next to King Alcinous at dinner. When he saw Demodocus arrive, he asked a servant to take the bard a plate of meat. Demodocus accepted it with pleasure, and Odysseus said, 'I have never heard music as beautiful as yours, Demodocus, and it is wonderful that you know the story of the Greeks' actions at Troy so well. Can you tell us now about another part of the war, when the Greeks built their wooden horse? If you sing of this as it really happened, I will tell the world of your god-given skill.'

The bard was happy to take this story as his subject. The wooden horse was, he sang, Odysseus's idea for getting Greek soldiers inside the walls of Troy. An enormous, hollow horse was made and Odysseus and some others hid inside. Then the rest of the Greeks burnt their defences and sailed away from the coast, pretending that they had given up the war. When the Trojans saw the horse, they pulled it through the gates of the city, but they argued about what to do next. Some wanted to throw it off a hillside and break it on the rocks below, but others wanted to keep it as a great gift to the gods. In the end the horse was left untouched. That night, Odysseus and his friends climbed out of the horse and opened the city gates to their army outside. Greek soldiers poured through the gates to destroy the city. They ran through the steep streets leaving death behind them, while Odysseus and Menelaus had the fight of their lives against the son of the Trojan king.

While the bard was singing, tears ran down Odysseus's face. When Alcinous noticed his guest's condition, he said, 'Phaeacians, though Demodocus tells his story beautifully, it does not please everyone in the room. Since we began our meal, our guest has been crying bitterly. Let us stop the story now, so that he can enjoy his last evening with us. We do not want to upset him.

'And sir, you should tell us now who you are. Where is your home? Our seamen will need to know where to take you. And tell us about your life and your travels. What places have you visited? What sights have you seen? And explain why our bard's stories of the Trojan War cause you so much unhappiness. Did you know someone who died at Troy? Did you lose a good friend, or someone from your family?'

3.1 Were you right?

Look at your answers to Activity 2.4. Then complete this diary.

The diary of

(1) _____

2) _____ told me to build
a raft. I sailed from her island and was
nearly at the land of the Phaeacians
when (3) _____ started a
storm. My raft was broken and I
had to swim to shore. Near the beach,
I met (4) _____ .

3.2 What more did you learn?

Whose thoughts are these? Who are they thinking about? Write 1–6 in the
boxes and write the missing names.

1 *I do not want to go.
I love him.*

4 *He is more attractive
than I first thought.*

2 *I am still very angry with
him. He hurt my son.*

5 *He would be a good husband
for my daughter.*

3 *She is very beautiful. She
will make someone a
lovely wife.*

6 *He knows a lot about the
Trojan War, but his
stories make me sad.*

a ☐ Odysseus, thinking about ....

b ☐ Nausicaa, thinking about ....

c ☐ Odysseus, thinking about ....

d ☐ 1 Calypso, thinking about .Odysseus...........................

e ☐ Poseidon, thinking about ....

f ☐ Alcinous, thinking about ....

3.3 **Language in use**

Look at the sentences in the box.
Then join the sentences below
with the words on the right.

> Laodamas, **who** had won the
> fighting, then went to Odysseus.
>
> He has nearly reached the land of
> the Phaeacians, **where** his suffering
> is going to end.

1   Hermes visited Calypso's island. Odysseus was living there.   where

....

....

2   Odysseus used Calypso's tools. She kept them in her cave.   which

....

....

3   Poseidon controlled the seas. He started a great storm.   who

....

4   Odysseus's raft was broken. He swam to shore.   whose

....

....

3.4 **What happens next?**

Look at the pictures and then write A, B or C below. What do you think?

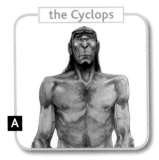
the Cyclops
A

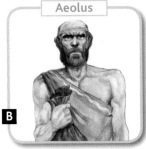
Aeolus
B

Circe
C

1   ☐ is the son/daughter of a god.   6   ☐ turns men into pigs.
2   ☐ is a god/goddess.   7   ☐ is blinded by Odysseus.
3   ☐ is a king/queen.   8   ☐ drinks too much wine.
4   ☐ controls the winds.   9   ☐ gives people a magic drink.
5   ☐ eats Odysseus's men.   10   ☐ helps Odysseus, but only once.

CHAPTER 5

A Monster with One Eye

*'He jumped up, caught two of my companions in his great hands,
and knocked their heads against the stone floor of the cave.'*

'**K**ing Alcinous,' said Odysseus, 'I do not know where to begin and end my story. The gods have put so many troubles in my path! But I shall start by giving you my name. Though my home is far from here, I want you all to think of me as your friend. I am Odysseus, son of Laertes, and my home is on Ithaca. It is a rocky island, but there is no sweeter sight for a man than his own country. The whole world talks about my clever plans during the Trojan War. But let me tell you about the disastrous voyage that followed.

'From Troy, I sailed with my companions to the city of the Cicones, who had fought for the Trojans in the war. We destroyed the city and killed most of the men who lived there. We shared the women and the treasures from the city between us, and then I told my men to leave. The fools refused. There was still a lot of wine and meat in the city, so they stayed there, filling their stomachs. This gave the Cicones time to get help from other cities in the area, whose armies were larger and better trained. In the morning, they attacked us – as many of them as the leaves and flowers in spring. We held them back at first, but after a whole day of fighting they broke our line. My men and I had to run to our ships in confusion, with the enemy at our back. Six men from each of our twelve ships were killed. The rest of us were lucky to escape alive.

'We sailed away as fast as we could, crying for our lost companions. Soon there was more trouble. When we were nearly home, the winds carried us in the wrong direction, past Cythera. For nine days we were chased across the waves by those disastrous winds, and on the tenth day we reached the land of the **Lotus**-eaters. We got out of the ships, collected fresh water for the next part of our voyage, and had a quick meal on the beach. Then I sent three of my companions to find out what sort of people lived in this land.

'The men soon met the Lotus-eaters. Luckily, they were peaceful people who liked to share their lotus fruit with strangers. There was just one problem – if you ate this sweet fruit, you forgot all thoughts of home. Immediately, my companions had no wish to return to the ships and bring us news. They only wanted to stay with the Lotus-eaters and eat lotus fruit all day. In the end, I had to use force to bring them back. Tears ran down their faces as I tied them onto the ship and ordered the other men to continue the voyage home.

lotus /'ləʊtəs/ (n) a type of fruit that exists only in stories

'Next we came to the land of the Cyclopes. They are rough, lawless people, one-eyed and much taller than normal men. They have no form of government, but live with their families and their sheep in caves in the mountains, paying no attention to their neighbours. They live on good farm land, but they do not grow food on it. They have no ships, either, so know nothing of the outside world.

'We landed on an island not far from the Cyclopes's coast and had a look around. No one lived on the island, but there were plenty of animals and fruit for food, and a fresh-water stream. It was a perfect place to rest from our voyage. Some of the men went hunting, and soon there was meat cooking on the fires. All day we ate, washing down the food with red wine that we had taken from the Cicones. We looked across the sea to the land of the Cyclopes. We could see the smoke from their fires, and could even hear them calling to their sheep.

'The next morning, I called the men together. "My friends," I said, "I am going to take my ship to find out what kind of people live in that land over there. The rest of you, stay here and wait for our return."

'My crew sat at their oars and it was not long before we had crossed to the mainland. As we were making the ship safe on the beach, we noticed a cave close to the sea. It had a very tall entrance, and an area outside surrounded by a great wall of stones and branches. I chose my twelve best men to come with me, and told the rest of my loyal companions to guard the ship. I filled a large wineskin with the finest wine from the ship. It had been a present from one of the Cicones, a servant of the god Apollo, whose family I had protected during our attack on his city. It was a wonderful drink. The servant had kept it secret for many years, and when he drank it he mixed one cupful of wine with twenty cupfuls of water. The smell of the wine was heavenly, and no one could refuse a drink of it. I brought this wine with me, and some food, because I had a strange feeling that the people in this land were not going to be welcoming hosts.

'It did not take us long to reach the cave. Its owner was not at home, so we went inside and looked around. There were enormous baskets of cheese, wooden buckets full of milk, and sheep organised into different age groups – new-born babies in one area, spring-born in another, and summer-born in a third. My men suggested taking some cheese and sheep to the ship and sailing away quickly. Although this was good advice, I decided instead to wait for the owner of the cave to return. I was hoping for some gifts from our host.

'We lit a fire, ate some cheese, and sat down to wait. At last, the cave's owner arrived. He was a great **monster**, more like a mountain than a man, and had one big eye in the middle of his face. He was carrying an enormous pile of dry wood for the fire, which he threw down on the ground inside the cave with a great

monster /ˈmɒnstə/ (n) a large, ugly, frightening animal or person that exists only in stories

crash. We were so frightened by the noise that we ran to the back of the cave. He had been out on the hills with the adult sheep. Now he drove some of the sheep into the cave for milking, and left the others in the walled area outside. Then he closed the entrance with an enormous stone, too big for twenty horses to pull. He milked his sheep, then put each mother with her young. He used some of the milk for cheese, and left the rest in a bucket to drink with supper. When he had finished his work, he lit the fire again. That was the moment when he saw us.

'"Strangers!" he cried. "Who are you? Where are you from? And why have you come to these shores?"

'The man's monstrous body and deep, loud voice filled us with terror, but I managed to find the words to reply. "We are Greeks," I said, "on our way back from Troy. The winds drove us in the wrong direction – as the gods intended, I suppose. We are proud to say that we fought with great Agamemnon in the Trojan War. But now we are asking for your help. We are hoping that you can welcome us as your guests, and perhaps even give us some gifts. Remember your duty to Zeus, who is the protector of travellers in need of a friendly welcome."

'"Stranger, you must be a fool, or from very far from here, if you think that I care about Zeus and the other gods. We Cyclopes are much stronger than the gods. I will only be kind to you and your men if it suits me, not out of fear of Zeus's punishments. But tell me, where did you leave your ship? Was it near here, or further along the coast?"

'His question was intended to trick me, but I am not a fool. I quickly thought of a story to tell him. "Our ship was destroyed in a storm off your coast. It is in pieces on the rocks north of here. Luckily, I and my friends here escaped alive."

'The cruel monster did not reply. Instead, he jumped up, caught two of my companions in his great hands, and knocked their heads against the stone floor of the cave. He ate their legs first, then their arms, then the rest of them, even the bones, until there was nothing left. We watched in shock, praying to Zeus for pity. When the Cyclops had finished his meal and washed it down with milk, he stretched out next to his sheep for a sleep.

'I felt for my sword, planning to kill him as he slept. But then I saw the heavy stone in the entrance and realised that without his strength we could never get out of the cave. So we waited fearfully for morning.

'When he woke, the Cyclops lit the fire again and milked his sheep. Then he took two more of my men and ate them greedily. Finally, he pushed the stone away from the entrance without difficulty, drove the adult sheep out of the cave, and replaced the stone. As he went with the sheep to find grass, I was left in the cave with murder in my heart.

'This was my plan. In the cave there was an enormous stick. The Cyclops sometimes carried it when he was out walking, but it was big enough to support the sail of a good-sized ship. I cut off part of this stick and gave it a sharp point at the end. Then my men and I held it over the fire to make it hard. When it was ready, we hid it at the back of the cave. Then I chose four men to help me when the Cyclops returned.

'Evening finally came, and the Cyclops returned with his sheep. This time he left none of the sheep outside in the walled area. When they were all safely inside the cave with him, he closed the entrance with the stone, did the milking, took another two of my men and started eating. Trying to hide my fear, I went to him with a wooden bowl full of the wine that I had brought with me. "Here, Cyclops, have some wine to wash down your meal. There was some very fine wine on our ship. We brought it to you as a gift, hoping that you would help us on our journey home. We wanted to be your friends, but your treatment of us has been more terrible than we ever imagined. Are you not ashamed of your behaviour?"

'The Cyclops laughed and took the wine. It tasted so good that he drank it quickly and asked for more. "And while you pour it, tell me your name," he said. "I would like to give you a present too – something that you will really like. We Cyclopes have wine, too, but it is nothing compared to this drink of yours."

'I gave him another bowlful of wine, and he drank it even more quickly than before. Three times I filled the bowl for him, and three times the fool drank to the bottom of the bowl. Finally, when the wine had confused his mind, I said,

"Cyclops, you asked me my name. I will tell you, and then you can give me the gift that you have promised. My name is Nobody."

'The cruel monster answered, "And here is my gift. Of all these men, I will eat Nobody last."

'Soon after he said this, he fell to the ground. He did not get up, but lay on his back, laughing, until he went to sleep. In this alcoholic sleep, he was sick. Wine mixed with bits of my eaten men poured from his mouth. It was hard not to be sick ourselves at this terrible sight. But this was our moment to act. I put the end of our stick into the dying fire to make it hot. Just before the stick started to burn, I pulled it out of the fire. Then my companions and I drove the sharp point of the stick into the Cyclops's eye. With all our force, we held it there, as his eye smoked and burned. He gave a terrible scream, and we moved away in terror.

'He pulled the stick from his eye, which was pouring blood onto the ground. Throwing the stick away, he called to the other Cyclopes who lived in caves in the area. Hearing his screams, they came to find out what was wrong. From

outside the cave, they shouted, "What is the matter, Polyphemus? Why have you woken us all up with those screams and shouts of yours? Is someone stealing your sheep or trying to kill you?"

'Out of the cave came Polyphemus's reply. "My friends, Nobody is trying to kill me."

'"Well, if no one is attacking you and your sheep are safe, you must be crazy," said his neighbours. "Illnesses of the mind are sent by Zeus, so we can do nothing to help you. You should pray to your father, the god Poseidon."

'And his neighbours went home, while I laughed that my false name had tricked them so easily. The Cyclops was still crying out in pain. He felt around the mouth of the cave with his hands, hoping to catch us as we tried to escape. Did he really think that I was so stupid? But if we wanted to leave the land of the Cyclopes alive, we needed a good plan. I spent a long time thinking. In the end, this is what I decided to do.

'The male sheep in the cave were fine animals, big and strong with coats of thick black wool. I quietly tied these sheep together in groups of three, putting one of my men under the middle sheep in each group so that there was a sheep on either side to protect him. For myself I chose the biggest sheep of all. I held on to his wool and hung upside-down between his legs. We waited like this until morning.

'When it grew light, the sheep made their way to the mouth of the cave. Their master, although still in great pain, passed his hands over the backs of all the animals as they stopped in front of him. The fool never thought of looking under the sheep's chests, where my men were tied. My own sheep was the last one to reach the doorway; he walked more slowly than the others because of my heavy weight. As Polyphemus felt his back, he said, "Dear sheep, why are you the last to leave today? Usually you lead your companions proudly to the best grass and the clearest water in the stream, and return first in the evening to the cave. But today you are last of all. You must be sad about your master's eye. How cruel was the man who did this to me! Nobody was his name, and I will find a way to punish him. He is not safe yet. Ah, if you had a voice, you could tell me where to look for him. I would break open his head on the floor of the cave to pay him back for the pain that he has caused me!"

'With these words, he let the sheep pass through the mouth of the cave. When we were a safe distance from the Cyclops, I came out from under my sheep and untied my companions. Then we quickly drove the sheep down towards our ship. The men at the ship were very happy to see us, but their smiles soon disappeared when they heard of the terrible fate of our lost companions. Their loud crying was putting us all in danger, so I made them get the sheep onto the ship as quickly and quietly as possible. Then the crew sat at their oars and took the ship out to sea.

'Before we were too far from Polyphemus, I shouted, "Cyclops! Your strength could not protect you from the resourceful Greeks. This is your punishment for eating your guests."

'My words made the Cyclops so angry that he pulled a great rock from the mountainside and threw it at us. It fell just in front of our ship, causing a wave that sent us back towards the shore. With a long stick, I pushed us back out to sea, and the crew pulled hard on their oars to save us from disaster. When I started to shout at the Cyclops again, my men tried to stop me. "Why do you want to anger this monster?" they asked. "He nearly killed us with that last rock. The next one will certainly be the end of us."

'But I was too full of emotion to listen to their advice. "Cyclops!" I shouted again, "you should know the name of the man who blinded you. If anyone asks you, tell them that it was Odysseus, destroyer of cities, son of Laertes, who lives on the island of Ithaca."

'The Cyclops cried sadly, "So the prophecy was true! Long ago I was warned that a man called Odysseus would rob me of my sight. But I had always expected a powerful man, someone bigger and stronger than me. And here you are, a weak little man who confused my mind with wine and destroyed my eye. But come here, Odysseus, so that I can give you some gifts and ask Poseidon to protect you on your voyage home. Poseidon is my father, so he will listen to my request. He will give me back my sight, too, if that is my fate."

'I shouted in reply, "You are a fool, Cyclops. Poseidon will never mend your eye."

'The Cyclops held up his hands to the sky and prayed to his father. "Poseidon, hear your son's request. Stop Odysseus, son of Laertes, from reaching his home in Ithaca. That is my dearest wish. But if you cannot do this, at least give him a terrible journey. Kill his companions, destroy his ships, and cause trouble in his palace at home."

'The sea-god Poseidon was listening.

'Again, the Cyclops picked up a great rock – an even bigger one than before – and threw it with all his strength at our ship. This time, though, we were further from the shore; the rock fell behind us and its wave swept us forward to safety.

'At last, we reached the island where the rest of the men were waiting for our return. We shared the sheep equally between the twelve ships, but the men gave me the sheep that had carried me out of Polyphemus's cave. I sacrificed this fine animal to the great god Zeus. But Zeus was not interested in the sacrifice. He was already busy planning the death of all my loyal companions.'

CHAPTER 6

Circe

*'They had taken the shape of pigs. Their minds were still human,
but they could not speak; only pig noises came from their mouths.'*

'We sailed towards home, thinking sadly of the dead friends that we were leaving behind. Next we came to the island of Aeolia, the home of Aeolus and his twelve children – six daughters and six fine sons. Each son is married to one of the daughters, and they spend all their days with their parents, eating wonderful food from dishes of gold.

'For a whole month Aeolus entertained us. He wanted to know all about the war in Troy, the Greek army, and our return home. I told him everything that I could. I soon learnt that Zeus had given Aeolus control of the winds. He offered to help us on our journey by giving me a leather bag in which all the strong and stormy winds were kept prisoner. He put this bag carefully in my ship and tied it up tightly so that the winds had no chance of escape. Then he sent us on our way with a gentle wind from the west, which blew our ships safely towards home.

'For nine days we sailed east. I guided the ship home myself, without a minute's rest. Then, finally, our homeland came into view. We could even see people working outside their houses. At last I felt that I could relax, and fell into a deep sleep. While I slept, my crew started talking about the bag from Aeolus. "There must be a fortune in gold and silver in that bag," they said. "Odysseus is so greedy. He is going home rich, but we, who have travelled the same distances and lived through the same dangers, are returning with nothing. It is just not fair! Let us see how much treasure he has got in that bag."

'Without stopping to think, they untied the bag. Immediately the winds rushed out and a violent storm blew up. Our twelve ships were carried back out to sea, far away from our homes on Ithaca. The men were all crying when I woke up. When I realised what had happened, I nearly threw myself into the sea to end my life. But I stayed on the ship, and we were all driven back to the island of Aeolus.

'After a quick rest on the beach, I went with two companions to Aeolus's palace. When he saw us outside his hall, he cried, "Odysseus? What unlucky fate has brought *you* here again?"

'Sadly, I answered, "The stupidity of my crew and my own need for sleep have brought me back. Please, help me again. I am sure that this time my voyage will be successful."

'He was silent. Finally, he shouted, "Get off this island at once! It is not right for me to help a man who is so hated by the gods. Your arrival here proves that you have no friends on Mount Olympus. Leave now!"

'His words upset me deeply, but I left the palace as he ordered and returned to the ships. We sailed for home again, but with none of the good humour that went with us on our earlier voyage.

'After six days at sea, we reached the land of the Laestrygonians. There we found a great curve of beach circled by high walls of rock, with only a narrow entrance. The captains of the other ships sailed straight in and landed on the shore. I did not follow them. Instead, I tied my own ship to a rock just outside the entrance. We all climbed up the steep rocks to find out what kind of land we had come to. We saw no farms and no people, but there was some smoke in the distance. I sent three of my men in the direction of the smoke.

'They followed a path for some time, until they saw a big, strong girl carrying buckets of water into a town. When they asked her about her country's king, she pointed to the high roof of her father's home. She was the daughter of King Antiphates. The men entered the king's palace and met his wife, a woman as tall as a mountain. They stood still in terror as she called her husband from the city's meeting-place. When the enormous Antiphates arrived, he immediately caught one of my companions in his hands and ate him. The other two ran away, and managed to reach the ships.

'But Antiphates was soon at the coast with an army of monstrous Laestrygonians. Standing high above the beach, they threw rocks down at the ships and men on the shore. When the ships were all broken, they picked up the men one by one and ate them. The cries of the dying men were terrible, but I could do nothing to help them. My ship was beyond the entrance to the beach, safe from the monsters. My crew, fearing for their lives, pulled hard on their oars, and we were soon in the safety of the open sea. But that was the end of all the other ships.

'My crew and I travelled across the sea to the island of Aeaea. There we lay on the beach for two days, not eating or drinking, but thinking sadly about our lost companions. On the morning of the third day, I climbed a hill to look at the island. There was just one house, in the middle of a forest. I decided not to go there at once. Instead, I went hunting and returned to my men with some fresh meat.

'"My friends," I said to them, "disaster has followed disaster recently, but we are still alive. Get up and eat. There is no point in dying from hunger."

'They did as I advised, and when night came they were feeling a little stronger and more hopeful. The next morning, I called a meeting. "I will not lie to you, friends," I began. "We are completely lost. With all these clouds in the sky, we do not even know which way is east. We must make a sensible plan, but I do not know what to suggest. We are on an island, and there is a house in the middle of a forest. There is nothing else that I can tell you."

'At this news, the men lost all hope. They thought of the Laestrygonians and refused to visit any more strangers. But we had to find help from somewhere.

'In the end, I put the men into two groups. We said goodbye to each other with tears in our eyes, fearing that we would never meet again. My group stayed by the ships and Eurylochus led the other group into the forest. Between the trees, they soon found a house built of stone. Dangerous animals surrounded the house, but instead of attacking the men, they greeted them as a friendly dog greets its master. The men stopped, confused by this unusual behaviour.

'They could hear a woman singing inside the house. After a whispered discussion, the men decided to call out to her. She came quickly. She said that her name was Circe, and she invited them in. In their innocence, they followed her into the house. Only Eurylochus sensed the danger and stayed outside. Circe gave the rest of the men a wonderful meal. But she had added a magic drug to their drink. When the men finished, they saw that they had taken the shape of pigs. Their minds were still human, but they could not speak; only pig noises came from their mouths. Circe took a stick and drove them outside. There they sat in the mud, eating the pig food that she threw to them.

'After waiting near the house for several hours, Eurylochus ran back to the ship. In tears, he told us that none of his companions had reappeared after they had entered Circe's house. I picked up my sword and asked him to lead the way back there. He went down on his knees, crying, "No, Odysseus, please! Do not make me go with you. You cannot help the others, and you will not return yourself. It is better to sail away quickly with the men that are left."

'"Dry your tears, Eurylochus," I replied. "You can stay by the ship. But I must go – I have no choice."

'I walked into the forest alone. I was near Circe's house when I met Hermes, the messenger of the gods. He took my hand and said, "Where are you going now, Odysseus? Are you planning to free your friends from Circe's magic? Be careful! She has turned them into pigs. You are likely to suffer the same fate and never see your homeland again. But I can help you. This flower is a drug that will protect you from Circe's magic. Eat it now, and when she hits you with her stick, attack her with your sword. She will be very frightened and will immediately ask to be your friend. You should agree. But first make her promise not to trick you or drug you again."

'I ate the white flower that he gave me. Then I continued along the path to Circe's house. I stood outside and called. Circe heard me and invited me in. She gave me some of her magic drink, but because of Hermes's drug, it had no effect on me. She hit me with her stick and shouted, "Go and join your pig friends in the mud!" At that moment, I attacked her with my sword.

'She went down on her knees, screaming and crying, and said, "Who are you and where are you from? You are the only man who has ever had that magic drink and not suffered any ill effects. You must be Odysseus. Hermes has often warned me to expect you on your way back from Troy. But we should not be enemies. Let us be friends."

'"Circe," I replied, "how can we be friends when you have turned my companions into pigs? I will only agree if you promise not to trick me or drug me again."

'She promised, and so we went back inside. She gave me a bath, dressed me in new clothes and offered me more food. When she saw that I was not eating, she asked me what the matter was. "How can I eat," I replied, "when I do not know if my men are safe? There will be no pleasure for me in food and drink until I see my loyal companions again."

'Circe went outside at once, and came back with some smelly pigs covered in mud. She put a special cream on the head

44

of each one, and they magically turned into men again, but younger, taller and more handsome than before. We all cried tears of happiness. It was wonderful to see everyone safe and well.

'Circe now told me to fetch the rest of my men from the seashore. When they saw me, they greeted me with great excitement. They had been sure that I would never return. We pulled the ship onto dry land and hid our treasure and equipment in a cave. The men were in a hurry to see their friends at Circe's house, but Eurylochus stopped them. "Where are you going now, you fools?" he said to them. "Have you learned nothing from the past few weeks? Odysseus leads us from one disaster to another. It is because of his thoughtless love of adventure that our companions died in the Cyclops's cave."

'When I heard Eurylochus's words, I nearly cut his head from his body with my sword. But my men held me back. "Let Eurylochus stay here with the ship," they said. "The rest of us want to go with you to meet Circe."

'In the end, Eurylochus came too. He did not want to stay alone by the ship. So together we walked back to Circe's house and found our companions having baths. Everyone greeted each other with tears in their eyes. Then Circe ordered her servants to prepare a meal, and we celebrated our first evening at Circe's house in very good humour.'

4.1 Were you right?

Look back at your answers to Activity 3.4. Then write the names to complete this dictionary of characters from Greek literature.

> **1** .... A one-eyed monster who is the son of the sea-god Poseidon. He eats six of Odysseus's men, but is blinded by Odysseus when he drinks too much wine.
>
> **2** ....A goddess who turns Odysseus's men into pigs. She gives Odysseus her magical drink too, but he is protected against her magic.
>
> **3** .... The king of Aeolia, who controls the winds. He helps Odysseus on his journey home, but when Odysseus returns, he refuses to help a second time.

4.2 What more did you learn?

Correct these sentences.

1 Odysseus tells the Cyclops that his name is Nowhere.

....

....

2 Odysseus escapes from the Cyclops's cave in a box.

....

....

3 The Cyclopes destroy all except one of Odysseus's ships.

....

....

4 Odysseus's men open the bag from Aeolus because they think there is wind in it.

....

....

5 Athene gives Odysseus a flower to protect him from Circe's magic.

....

....

4.3 Language in use

**Look at the sentences on the right.
Then report these sentences in
the same way.**

> 'My name **is** Circe,' she said.
>
> She said that **her** name **was** Circe.

1   'We are returning from Troy,' Odysseus told him.

    Odysseus told him that …they were returning from Troy……………… .

2   'Odysseus has been very cruel to me,' the Cyclops shouted.

    The Cyclops shouted that ……………………………………………………………

    ………………………………………………………………………………………… .

3   'Circe will use her magic on you,' Hermes warned Odysseus.

    Hermes warned Odysseus that …………………………………………………

    ………………………………………………………………………………………… .

4   'Circe invited us into her house,' said Eurylochus.

    Eurylochus said that ……………………………………………………………………

    ………………………………………………………………………………………… .

5   'You can stay in my house for the winter,' Circe told them.

    Circe told them that ……………………………………………………………………

    ………………………………………………………………………………………… .

4.4 What happens next?

Look at the pictures in Chapter 7.

At the end of the chapter, Odysseus is the only member of the crew left alive. Guess
what happens to his men. Make notes.

Notes

Teiresias's Prophecy

*'If you leave his cows unharmed, you will arrive safely in Ithaca.
But if you hurt those cows, your ship and your men will be destroyed.'*

'Circe was a very welcoming hostess, and we stayed with her for a whole year. But as the months passed and the long days of summer returned, my companions became anxious that I had forgotten my home in Ithaca. "Why are we still here on Circe's island?" they asked me one day. "It is time to continue our voyage."

'That night I spoke to Circe. I told her about my companions' complaints, and she agreed to help us with our voyage. "But first," she said, "you must visit the Underworld and talk to blind old Teiresias. Although he is dead, his prophecies are as true as they were during his lifetime."

'This news broke my heart. I nearly chose to end my life there in Circe's house to escape the awful journey to the world of the dead. But finally I asked her, "How can I find the way? No one has ever sailed a ship into Hell."

'"Do not worry. The north wind will blow you to the right place. At the edge of the world, you will see a place where tall trees grow. Land your ship there and the ghosts of the Underworld will come to you."

'She told me what to do and say when I reached that terrible place. She promised that Teiresias would tell me the route of my journey home.

'Waking everyone up in the morning, I shouted, "Hurry, my friends, and say goodbye to your comfortable beds. It is time to go. Circe has given us instructions for the next part of our journey."

'My brave companions were happy to make their way back to the ship. But even this time I did not lead everyone away safely. Elpenor was the youngest in our group, and not very clever. The night before, after too much wine, he had decided to sleep on the roof because the air was fresher there. Woken in the morning by the noise of our departure, he jumped up suddenly and fell off the roof. The fall broke his neck. When we went to help him, we found him dead.

'By the ship, I told the men that our voyage would not take us straight home. When they heard that our destination was the world of the dead, they were filled with terror. But they could say nothing to change the fate that the gods had chosen for us.

'Circe gave us a good wind to fill our sails and, a day after leaving Aeaea, we reached a dark land at the edge of the world. There we found the place that Circe had described, where tall trees grow. I landed the ship and started to follow Circe's instructions for calling the dead. I dug a hole in the ground, the size of a man's arm. Into this hole I poured milk, water and sweet wine. I prayed to the dead and sacrificed two fine sheep from my ship. As their blood poured into the hole, ghosts started to come up from the earth – young girls, old men, and soldiers killed in war. They were making a strange noise, and cold fear ran through me. I guarded the hole with my sword held tightly. I did not want any ghosts to get to the blood before Teiresias.

'Suddenly, I recognised the ghost of Elpenor. In our hurry to leave Circe's island, we had not burnt his body or built a mound of earth for him. I called out, "Elpenor! You have reached here more quickly on foot than we did in our fast ship."

'"Yes, master, but you rushed away from Aeaea too fast. Please, when you return, remember my body. Burn it on the beach with my sword, and build a mound of earth in my memory. At the top, plant the oar that I used on the ship with my dear companions."

'"I will do all that you ask, dear Elpenor," I replied.

'Teiresias was not far behind him.

'"Odysseus, son of Laertes, why have you left the sunlight to visit the dead in this sad, dark place? If you want a prophecy, step away from the blood. I will tell you your future after I have drunk."

'I let him drink the blood, and he soon said, "My lord Odysseus, you want an easy route home. But Poseidon is angry about your cruel treatment of his son, the Cyclops, and he is going to make your journey hard. You and your men will finally reach home, though, if you can control your hunger when you come to the island of Thrinacie. There you will find the fat cows of the Sun-god, who can see everything on his daily journey across the sky. If you leave his cows unharmed, you will arrive safely in Ithaca. But if you hurt those cows, your ship and your men will be destroyed.

'"You yourself will return home on a foreign ship and find your family in terrible trouble. You will find arrogant suitors in your palace, eating your food and demanding marriage with your wife. You will kill the suitors for their crimes. But then you must start another journey. Take an oar and travel until you find a place where the people know nothing about the sea and ships and the use of salt in their food. You will meet a man who calls your oar a farm tool. That will be your sign. Plant your oar in the earth and sacrifice a sheep, a cow and a pig to the great god Poseidon. After this, you can go home. You will have a long life, and you will die peacefully of old age, far from the terrors of the sea."

'"So this is the fate that the gods have chosen for me," I said. "Thank you, Teiresias."

'As Teiresias went back to the Underworld, the ghost of my mother, Anticleia, came towards me. I was deeply upset to see her there. She had been alive when

I left Ithaca for the war in Troy. "Mother, tell me what happened to you," I cried. "What death brought you to this terrible place?"

"'It was sadness that killed me, Odysseus, my child. I missed your wise and gentle ways, and life gave me no pleasure. In death, I have escaped that pain."

'I tried to put my arms around her, but there was nothing to hold. My arms went straight through her.

"'You cannot touch me, Odysseus. When life leaves the body, we become no more than a dream. But go now, return to the world of the sun, and find your way back home."

"'But what can you tell me about home," I asked her. "How is the rest of the family? Are they safe and well?"

"'Penelope and Telemachus are still living in your palace, trying to keep your lands safe from the greedy suitors. But your father Laertes lives a sad and lonely life, alone on his fruit farm. He never goes down to the city now. In winter he sleeps on the floor by his fire, without a bed or a blanket to keep him warm. In summer, he sleeps under the fruit trees in a bed of leaves. As old age presses down on him, he thinks of nothing except your return."

'Soon Persephone, Queen of the Underworld, drove away my mother and the other women ghosts who were with her. In shock, I saw another ghost that I recognised – Agamemnon. He drank the dark blood and stretched out his hand towards me. But all the strength had left the body that had been so powerful, and he could not reach me. He and I looked at each other with tears in our eyes. Finally, I said, "Great king, what terrible fate has brought you here? Were you killed in a storm on your way home from Troy, or in a fight on enemy lands?"

'"No, my friend," Agamemnon replied. "I was murdered when I reached my homeland by my cousin Aegisthus. Aegisthus welcomed me to my palace, then killed me like a sheep for a sacrifice. My companions were cut down too, and the floor of the hall swam with blood. You saw the deaths of many fine men at Troy, Odysseus, but none were as pitiful as ours.

'"And, worst of all, my wife Clytaemnestra was there watching. When I was dying, with a sword in my chest, she turned away coldly and joined her lover, Aegisthus. She did not even close my eyes or mouth for me in death."

'"Poor man!" I cried. "Zeus has been a cruel enemy to your family, using the tricks of women to destroy your happiness. Your brother's wife Helen caused the Trojan War, and now your own wife has sent you here."

'"Yes," replied Agamemnon. "Never tell a woman all your secrets, Odysseus, not even your wife, because one day she may turn against you. When you reach home, do not sail openly into port. Hide your return until you are sure that you are safe. But you are luckier than I was, my friend. Your own wife, Penelope, has a loyal heart and a wise head."

'I said a sad goodbye to Agamemnon. I had learned what I needed to in this terrible place. It was time to leave.

'I called to my men to get the ship ready, and soon we were on our way. With a good wind in our sails, we quickly reached Aeaea, the island of beautiful Circe. We found Elpenor's body and took it to the highest place on the coast. There we built a fire and placed his body on it. We watched sadly as the flames surrounded him. When the fire was dead, we covered the place with a mound of earth and planted Elpenor's oar on top. I prayed that his death would be the last on our journey home.

'Circe had noticed our return, and came now with her servants, carrying bread, meat and wine. We had a good meal on the beach, in preparation for our voyage the next day. When it grew dark, my men went to sleep by the ship, but Circe held me back. She wanted to warn me about the dangers of the voyage ahead. "Listen to my advice, Odysseus, and hopefully you will remember it when you need it most. You will soon meet the Sirens. They sit on their island, singing to the sailors who pass. They ask people to come closer, and their voices are so beautiful that the sailors cannot refuse. But be careful. Piles of dead bodies lie all around that island. Its rocks destroy any ship that goes near.

'"But it is possible to sail past safely. Put **wax** in the ears of your crew, so that they cannot hear the Sirens' magical song. If you wish to hear it yourself, your men must tie you tightly to the ship. They must not free you until the danger has passed.

---

wax /wæks/ (n) something made of fat or oil, which is soft when it is warm; liquid *wax* is used to make furniture shine

'"When the Sirens are behind you, you will have to choose between two routes. One takes you to the Moving Rocks, which crash together whenever a ship sails between them. Even the birds cannot fly through this place safely, but lose a wing or a tail when the rocks squeeze tight. For sailors, there is no hope of escape.

'"In the other direction lie two rocks. One is so tall and steep that no one could climb to the top of it. Half way up there is a cave, and this is the home of the monster Scylla. She is a terrible sight, with twelve feet and six long necks, each ending in a head full of teeth as sharp as knives. She lies in her cave, stretching her long necks down to the sea in search of seals and fish to eat. No crew has ever passed her without losing men. She always catches a sailor in each of her six mouths.

'"The other rock is not as high, and is only a short distance across the water from Scylla's cave. A fruit tree grows from the rock, and below it the awful Charybdis pulls down the dark water to the sea floor. Three times a day she pulls it down, and three times she throws it up again. I pray that the gods keep you away from her, because not even the sea-god Poseidon could save your ship from her violent seas. No, you must stay close to Scylla's rock and sail past as quickly as you can. It is better to lose six of your men than your whole crew."

'"Yes," I replied. "But is there really no way to protect all my men from these two monsters?"

'"Are you still looking for trouble, Odysseus, after all that you have suffered? Scylla is a monster of great power. She cannot die. You will waste time if you try to fight her. Then she will be able to take even more of your men. No, you must accept your fate. Sacrifice six of your men and the rest will be safe."

'As she finished speaking, the sun came up. I said goodbye to Circe and went back to my companions. We untied the ship and were soon on our way. We made good progress as the men pulled on their oars. It was time to prepare them for the danger ahead.

'"My friends, Circe has given me advice for the rest of our journey. I must share it with you. First, we will come to the island of the Sirens. I will protect your ears from the magic of the Sirens' song. But one of us should listen. Tie me very tightly to the ship so that I cannot escape. If I complain, tie me more tightly. Do not take the ship near the island, even if I command it a hundred times. The rocks destroy all ships that go near."

'I took some wax and made it warm in my hands. Then I pushed a little into everyone's ears, so that they could hear nothing. When this was done, the men tied my hands and feet to the ship, and we were ready to continue.

'The Sirens' island soon came into view. We saw three strange women on the island, with beautiful human faces but the bodies of birds. They started their magical song, and it was the most beautiful music in the world. I was filled with desire to hear more. When they asked me to come to them, I wanted to with all my heart. I ordered my men to untie me, but of course they could not hear. I tried to break free, but they tied me more tightly. Sadly, I watched the men take me further and further from the Sirens' island. Finally, they untied me and took out the wax from their ears. With Circe's help, we were safe.

'But there was no time to discuss what had happened. We saw rough water ahead, and heard the thunder of waves against rocks. The crew were so frightened that the oars fell from their hands. I walked around the ship, saying, "We have met trouble before, my friends. With my help, you escaped the Cyclops's cave. Today you must follow my orders again. We are going to go as close as possible to the higher rock, keeping the ship away from the rough water. Stay at your oars and pull as hard as you can."

'The crew obeyed. I did not tell them about Scylla, because fear of the monster would stop them from pulling on their oars. I stood at the front of the ship, hoping to get the first view of those six long necks. I looked until my eyes grew tired, but I could see nothing.

'Then, suddenly, Charybdis threw up the water from the deep sea floor. Salt water fell down on us like rain, and the top of the sea was like boiling water. Then she pulled the water down again, and we could see the sand at the bottom of the sea.

'My men were pale with fear. Then, while everyone was looking at Charybdis, Scylla stretched her necks down from her cave and caught six of my strongest men in her mouths. Their arms and legs waved pitifully in the air as they called for help. But we could do nothing to save them. In seconds, the monster had carried them up to her cave and started her terrible meal.

'We continued sadly on our way, and soon we saw the lovely island of Thrinacie. As we came near the beach, we could heard the sound of cows. I remembered the words of Teiresias and said, "Listen carefully, my friends. In the Underworld, Teiresias warned me about this island. There is a greater danger here than any that we have met before. Sail past the island. We should not land."

'My men were very upset. Eurylochus shouted, "Do you never get tired, Odysseus? How can you tell us not to land here, after everything that has happened today? You must be made of iron! It is nearly sunset, and we are tired and hungry. If we continue past this island, we will be at sea all night – there is no other land near here. And storms are always worse at night. Do you really want the winds to destroy our ship? You are crazy. We should land here and cook our supper. In the morning, we can go back to the open sea."

'The rest of the crew agreed with him, and I realised that the gods had already decided our fate. "I am one against many, Eurylochus. I cannot refuse your demands. But I ask every one of you to promise that you will not harm the animals on the island. Sit peacefully and eat the food that Circe has given us. If you eat anything else, I cannot save you from a disastrous end."

'When everyone on the ship had given me their promise, we landed on the Sun-god's island. We ate a good supper, but the conversation kept returning to the men that Scylla had taken from us. During the night, a storm blew up, and in the morning it was not safe to sail. I called my companions to a meeting and said, "We still have plenty of food on the ship. Keep your hands off the cows on this island, or disaster will follow. They belong to the Sun-god, who can see everything on his daily journey across the sky."

'The men agreed willingly. But the storm did not stop. For a whole month it blew, and we were unable to leave the island. While our bread and wine lasted, the men obeyed my orders. When there was nothing more to eat, they went fishing and caught birds from the trees, but they were still hungry. I hoped that one of the gods would take pity on us and show me a way to escape. I found a quiet place, out of the wind, to pray. But when I had finished, the gods sent me into a deep sleep.

'While I slept, Eurylochus was causing trouble down by the ship. "No death is pleasant," he argued, "but a death from hunger is the worst. I say we should eat those cows. We can sacrifice them to the gods, and promise to give all our treasure to the Sun-god when we return to Ithaca. If he is still angry with us, let him destroy our ship. A quick death at sea is easier than a slow and painful one on this island."

'The rest of the crew agreed to his plan. Quickly, they brought the cows together and sacrificed them to the gods. They had no wine to pour over the meat as it cooked, so they used seawater instead.

'As I woke from my sleep, I smelled the meat cooking on the fire. "So the gods have decided to ruin me," I cried. "There is no hope for us now!"

'High in the sky, the Sun-god had seen my companions' crime. He went to Zeus in anger, saying, "Odysseus and his followers have killed my fine cows. You must punish them as they deserve. If you leave their actions unpunished, I will disappear from the sky and shine on the dead in the Underworld."

'"Shine on us here on Olympus and on the world of men," Zeus replied. "You can be sure that I will punish the criminals."

'This was their conversation on Olympus. Calypso heard about it from Hermes and later reported it to me.

'Down on the Sun-god's island, the men were frightened. They could already see the signs of the gods' anger. The skins of the dead animals were moving magically around the beach, and the pieces of meat on the fire were calling out to each other like cows. But we could do nothing to change the situation. The cows were dead. The damage had been done.

'For six days, the men ate the meat of the Sun-god's cows. On the seventh, the wind dropped and it was safe to sail. With fear in our hearts, we took our ship out to sea. Almost immediately, a cloud formed above the ship, making a dark shadow on the sea around us. Then came the wind. With the force of a wild animal, it attacked us. It pulled the sail from the ship in seconds. Wood came crashing down onto the sailors below and one man was knocked into the sea. Worse followed, as Zeus struck the ship with lightning. The whole ship shook violently. The men held on tightly, but one by one they were thrown from the ship. They were pulled this way and that in the water until they went down under the waves forever.

'I alone was left on board. But soon the strength of the enormous waves broke the ship into pieces. Luckily, I managed to climb onto a broken piece of wood, and I held on tightly. All night I was blown around by the wind. At sunrise I saw that I had been driven back to the rocks of Scylla and Charybdis. Charybdis was beginning to pull the waters down and I was swept towards a great hole in the sea. Just in time, I managed to catch a branch of the tree that grew from the rock. I could not get my feet onto the tree, but I hung by my arms, hour after hour. Finally, my wait was over. Charybdis threw up the wood that had saved me from the storm. I let myself fall back into the sea, swam to the wood and climbed back on. Luckily, Scylla did not see me, because there was nothing to protect me from her greedy mouths.

'I was at sea for another nine days, until the waves carried me to the shores of Calypso's island. She was kind to me and gave me a home. But I have already told you about my life with Calypso, good Phaeacians. I have reached the end of my story.'

CHAPTER 8

Coming Home

*'Look around you, Odysseus. Do you not recognise this beach,
those rocks, and that tree on the hills above?'*

When Odysseus had finished, the hall was silent until Alcinous said, 'Odysseus, you have suffered greatly. But I am sure that you will reach home safely now, with our help.'

Then he spoke to his Phaeacian guests. 'Friends,' he said, 'we have already given our guests fine gifts, but does this man not deserve more after all his troubles? Go now and bring him some more treasure from your home. Later we will ask the common people to pay for these gifts; we do not want any man's generosity to ruin him.'

The next day the Phaeacians came to the port with their gifts of gold and silver, and Alcinous himself helped to put the gifts safely on the ship. Then they all returned to the palace for more food and music, as the voyage was not going to start until sunset. All day Odysseus kept looking at the sun. He was like a farmer who has worked hard in the fields all day; sunset is a welcome sight to a man with tired legs and an empty stomach – it is the time to stop work and go home for supper. In the same way, Odysseus welcomed sunset that day. As soon as the sun had sunk below the sea, he said, 'Alcinous, great king, let me say goodbye. You have given me the two things that I most wanted – valuable gifts and a crew to take me home. I pray that the gods bring you and your family all the happiness that you deserve, and keep your people safe from harm.'

Odysseus and the Phaeacians walked down to the port, and the servants carried bread and wine for the voyage. On the ship, a blanket was spread out for Odysseus to sleep on. Then, after praying to the gods, Odysseus climbed on board. He lay down on the blanket and the crew sat at their oars. As the ship left the port, Odysseus immediately fell into a deep and peaceful sleep.

And now, like a team of four horses in a chariot race, the ship raced through the water towards Ithaca. After a journey of magical speed, it arrived on the coast of Ithaca just before sunrise. The crew found a beach with a large cave beside it. There the Phaeacian oarsmen landed the ship and lifted Odysseus, still asleep, onto the sand. They took all his gifts from the ship and piled them next to him. Then they started their voyage home.

Athene threw a fog over the island of Ithaca, so that no one noticed Odysseus before she could warn him of the dangers in his palace. As a result, when Odysseus woke up he did not recognise his homeland. He jumped to his feet and cried, 'Oh no! Whose country have I come to this time? Will they be kind hosts, or dangerous monsters? Where can I keep my treasure safe? And what were those dishonest Phaeacians thinking? They promised that they would take me home to Ithaca, but instead they have left me in this strange place. Let Zeus punish them for breaking their promise. I should look at my treasure too, to check that they have not stolen anything.'

He checked his gifts carefully, but none were missing. Just then, Athene came to him, disguised as a good-looking young farmworker. Odysseus was very happy to see that the people of the island were not monsters, and said, 'Good morning, friend. You are the first person that I have met in this land. Please help me. I need to find a safe place for my treasure. And I need to know where I am.'

'I am surprised that you do not know this land. It is famous in countries far west and far east of here. It is rocky – not a good place for horses – but it has good farmland and produces fine sheep and cows. Yes, even far away in Troy they know the name of Ithaca.'

Odysseus's heart filled with happiness when he heard that lovely name, but just in time he remembered to be careful.

'Of course,' he replied, 'even in Crete we have heard of Ithaca. Crete has been my home until now. But the king's son tried to take from me all the treasure that I won at Troy. It was very unfair. I had only one choice – to kill him. But when he was dead, I could not live safely in Crete. So I took the first ship that I could find. We were aiming for Pylos, but the wind was too strong and we were driven here instead. Last night we slept on this beach. When I woke in the morning, the ship and its crew had gone.'

Athene smiled at Odysseus's story, then changed into her true form. Odysseus stared in wonder at the beautiful goddess in front of him. 'So even in your homeland you have not given up your tricks, Odysseus! You and I are so similar. You are the cleverest and most resourceful person in the world of men, and I am the cleverest and most resourceful of the gods. But, though you are clever, you did not realise that the goddess Athene was beside you through all your adventures. I made the Phaeacians look after you kindly. And now I will help you again.'

'It is hard to recognise you in all your disguises, great goddess,' Odysseus replied. 'I remember your kindness at Troy, but have I really had much help from you since then? Where were you when the Greek ships were separated because of arguments and storms? Where were you when my companions were lost at sea?'

'You must understand that I could not act against Poseidon, who was very angry about your treatment of his son, the Cyclops.'

'But tell me, goddess, and I pray that you answer me honestly: is this really Ithaca, or were your words intended to make me suffer even more?'

'Look around you, Odysseus. Do you not recognise this beach, those rocks, and that tree on the hills above?'

As she spoke, she lifted the fog that was hiding the land from view. Odysseus recognised it at last. He threw himself down on the ground and kissed the sand.

'Come,' said the goddess. 'We must hide your treasure in that cave over there.' When everything was safely in the cave, Athene warned him about the situation in the palace. 'Penelope is surrounded by suitors. They are arrogant and greedy men, who will do anything. They are even trying to murder your son Telemachus. When it is time to fight them, I will be at your side,' she said. 'But at the moment they must not know about your return. I will disguise you as a man so old and poorly dressed that even your wife will not recognise you. Go and stay with Eumaeus, the pig farmer. He is still loyal to you and Penelope, and he loves Telemachus like a son. He can give you the news from the town. And I will bring Telemachus home from Sparta, where he has been asking Menelaus for news of you.'

Athene used her magic to change Odysseus into a weak old man. His skin hung loose on his body, his hair was white, and his clothes were dirty pieces of cloth. Then she disappeared suddenly, hurrying to Telemachus in Sparta.

◆

Odysseus followed a path up to the hills and the home of Eumaeus, the pig
farmer, the most loyal of all Odysseus's farmworkers. He found Eumaeus near
his hut, busy with his pigs. There were eight hundred on his farm, although their
number was reduced every day by the enormous meals at the palace.

The guard dogs saw Odysseus first and ran towards him. Luckily, Eumaeus
called them back before they attacked the stranger. 'Those dogs almost pulled
you to pieces, old man,' he said. 'Then I would have even more worries. The
situation is bad enough now. I spend my days making my master's pigs fat so that
other men can eat them. But my good, kind master is probably dying of hunger,
lost in a foreign land, or perhaps already dead. But come inside. When you have
had some food and wine, you can tell me about yourself.'

Inside the hut, Eumaeus offered his guest a seat on a pile of sticks with a
sheepskin thrown over it. 'Thank you for this warm welcome,' said Odysseus. 'I
hope that the gods are kind to you.'

Eumaeus prepared some simple food and gave it to Odysseus, saying, 'It is
not much, I am afraid. But we have little left after we have sent all our best pigs

to those arrogant men in the palace. They want to marry my absent master's wife, but they do not behave like future husbands. Instead, they sit around the palace all day. They kill several pigs every night and drink my master's wine like water. They must know that my master will never return, because they fear no punishment for their unlawful behaviour.'

Odysseus ate the food gratefully, thinking about what he would do to those suitors. When he had finished, he asked, 'So who is your absent master? You seem to have a very good opinion of him. Perhaps I have met him on my travels.'

'His name is Odysseus. It *was* Odysseus, I should say, because he is now lying dead somewhere. He was the kindest of masters and the best of men. He owned land here on Ithaca and on the mainland. He was rich in pigs and cows and sheep, and in treasure too. But the suitors are destroying his property day by day, and soon there will be nothing left. My heart aches when I think of it. But tell me, stranger, who *you* are. What has brought you to this island?'

Odysseus told him that he had been a prince of Crete. He had had an argument with his brother and had to leave his homeland. After many years of travel and a lot of bad luck, he now owned nothing in the world except the clothes that he was wearing. 'I met Odysseus once,' he added. 'He stayed at our palace in Crete on the way to Troy. And a few days ago I heard talk of him again. There was a ship in Thesprotia waiting to carry him home. The crew were expecting to start their voyage this week.'

'I am sorry for all your troubles, old man,' the pig farmer replied. 'But I cannot believe your story about Odysseus. Why are you telling such lies? Another man told me a similar story last year, and travellers regularly upset Penelope with false information. Odysseus never arrives, and only a fool now believes that he will.'

'If my story proves false, you can throw me from the highest rock on this island,' said Odysseus.

'Zeus would soon punish a man who invited a stranger into his home and then killed him for lying,' replied Eumaeus.

They spent the evening in friendly conversation in front of the fire. When it was time for sleep, Eumaeus lent Odysseus a thick coat to use as a blanket. Then, always careful of his master's property, he went out to sleep with the pigs, to protect them from thieves and wild animals during the night.

5.1 Were you right?

Look back at your answers to Activity 4.4. Then complete the sentences with these words.

Six	None (x2)	All the others

1 .... of Odysseus's men are killed by the Sirens.

2 .... are killed by Charybdis.

3 .... are killed by the monster Scylla.

4 .... are killed when the ship is struck by lightning.

5.2 What more did you learn?

Circle the <u>two</u> correct endings for each sentence.

1 Teiresias tells Odysseus about:

   a the sun-god's cows.

   b his mother's death.

   c another journey that he must make.

2 In the Underworld, Odysseus meets:

   a Agamemnon.

   b his mother.

   c his father.

3 Odysseus's men kill the cows on Thrinacie because:

   a they are hungry.

   b they do not know that it is wrong.

   c Odysseus is asleep and cannot tell them to stop.

4 When Odysseus arrives back in Ithaca, he:

   a does not recognise it.

   b is helped by Athene.

   c realises that the Phaeacians have stolen his treasure.

5 Eumaeus is:

   a rich.

   b a pig farmer.

   c kind.

5.3 **Language in use**

Look at the sentences on the right. Then rewrite these sentences with *let* or *make*.

> I **let** him **drink** the blood.
>
> Were your words intended to **make** me **suffer** even more?

1 'Odysseus can return home now,' Zeus said.

   Zeus .... let Odysseus return .... home.

2 'You have to visit the Underworld,' Circe told Odysseus.

   Circe .... the Underworld.

3 'You must land on the island,' the crew told Odysseus.

   The crew .... on the island.

4 'You can travel in our ship,' the Phaeacians said to Odysseus.

   The Phaeacians .... in their ship.

5.4 **What happens next?**

Match the questions with four of the names. What do you think?

the suitor Antinous   Telemachus
Penelope   the suitor Eurymachus
the old servant Eyrucleia   Eumaeus

1 Who does Odysseus first tell the news of his return to?

   ....

2 Who recognises Odysseus from a scar on his leg?

   ....

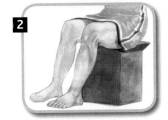

3 Which two people throw chairs at Odysseus?

   ....

CHAPTER 9

Telemachus Returns

'I am not a god,' replied Odysseus. 'But I am your father,
who has been the cause of so many problems for you.'

Athene now went to Sparta and found Telemachus and Peisistratus in the palace of King Menelaus. Peisistratus was asleep, but Telemachus was lying awake, worrying about his absent father and the problem of the suitors.

Athene stood near him and said, 'Go back to your palace and keep it safe from the greedy suitors. Your mother's father has told her to marry Eurymachus, since he is the richest of her suitors. If you do not go home soon, you will return to an empty house. But be careful. The suitors have sent a ship to attack you on your voyage home. They are waiting for you between Ithaca and the coast of Samos, with swords in their hands and murder in their hearts. Make sure that you go home a different way, and sail at night so that they cannot see your ship. Get off the ship at a quiet part of the coast and go straight to Eumaeus's pig farm, while your crew sail to the port and spread the news of your return.'

When she had delivered her message, she went back to Mount Olympus.

Telemachus woke Peisistratus with a gentle kick and said, 'Come, my friend, we must get the chariot ready and be on our way.'

'We should leave soon, I agree, Telemachus. But it is the middle of the night. We cannot drive in complete darkness, and what would Menelaus think if we rushed away like thieves in the night? Can our journey not wait until morning?'

Telemachus agreed to stay in Sparta for a few more hours. When daylight came, he went to speak to his host. 'Menelaus,' he said, 'I must go home. But I will never forget your kindness to me.'

'I will not keep you here against your wishes,' replied the king. 'But give me time to bring you some gifts. And enjoy one last meal with us before you leave.'

Menelaus gave him the bowl of fine silver that he had promised him the day before. Queen Helen added a present of her own. 'I made this dress myself,' she told Telemachus. 'It is for your future wife to wear on your wedding day.'

They then had some food, and after the meal Telemachus and Peisistratus climbed into their chariot.

'Goodbye, young friends,' said Menelaus. 'Give my good wishes to Nestor.'

'We will,' replied Telemachus. 'I only hope that one day I can give your good wishes to my father too, and tell him of your kindness to me.'

As he spoke, an eagle flew across the sky, carrying a chicken from a local farm in its feet. Some farmworkers were chasing the eagle, but it gave a cry and flew out to sea, far beyond their reach.

'This was a sign from the gods,' said Helen. 'And its message seems clear. Just as the eagle attacked the chicken, Odysseus will attack the suitors when he finds his way home. Or perhaps he is already in Ithaca, planning their death.'

'I pray that you are right,' said Telemachus. And with a shout to the horses, he started the chariot.

After a smooth journey, they reached Pylos the next day. Telemachus said goodbye to Peisistratus at the port. 'I am sorry that I cannot say goodbye to your father too. But I have no time to go to the palace. I need to get home urgently.'

As the crew carried the gifts from Menelaus onto the ship, a stranger came to Telemachus. 'Can you take me with you?' he asked. 'In Argos, my homeland, I have enemies who are trying to kill me. I think they have followed me here.'

'You are welcome to come with us,' replied Telemachus. 'We are going to Ithaca, and there you can stay as my guest.'

'I am grateful for your kindness, good friend,' said the stranger. 'My name is Theoclymenus. In Argos I am a famous prophet.'

They all climbed on board, and the crew pulled on their oars until Pylos was far behind them. In open sea, they put up the sail and the wind carried them quickly towards Ithaca. As Telemachus stared out at the waves, he wondered what would happen at the end of the voyage. Would he get home alive, or would the suitors succeed in their plan to murder him?

At the same time, Odysseus was having supper with Eumaeus in the hut. Wanting to test his host's loyalty, he said, 'I cannot take advantage of your kindness any longer. Tomorrow I will go to town and ask for work at the palace. And I can tell Queen Penelope that her husband will soon be home.'

'No, no!' replied Eumaeus. 'Penelope has listened to too many stories about Odysseus already. You would do no good. You would just upset her. And the suitors in the palace will not want *you* as their servant. They are surrounded only by good-looking young men with oil in their hair and handsome clothes. You might die a violent death if you went to the palace in search of work. No, it is better to stay here with me. When my master's son, Telemachus, returns from Pylos, he will give you some new clothes and send you wherever you want.'

'Your kindness continues, Eumaeus,' said his guest. 'I will wait for Telemachus's return as you suggest. But tell me, while I am here, about your master's family. Does he have a father or mother still living?'

'His father, Laertes, is still alive, but life brings him no happiness. He lost his son when Odysseus went to Troy, and then his dear wife died of a broken heart because of Odysseus's absence. She was a lovely woman. She was like a mother to me when I first came to Ithaca – I grew up in her house.'

'So you were still quite young when you came to Ithaca,' said Odysseus. 'What happened to you? How were you separated from your home and family?'

'Well, I was born in the far land of Syrie. My father, Ctesius, was its king. One day a ship arrived from Phoenicia with lots of jewels and pretty things for sale. One of my father's servants was Phoenician. As a young girl, she had been stolen from her homeland by criminals. Now she was a tall, beautiful woman, good at her work, but not very sensible. Well, this servant fell in love with one of the Phoenician sailors. He offered to take her home with him to Phoenicia and she was very excited at the idea. But to pay for her voyage the sailors asked her to steal some gold from my father's palace. She agreed willingly, saying, "There is something else that I can give you too. At the palace I look after my master's young son. He is a clever boy and he follows me everywhere. If I brought him too, you could sell him for a high price at any foreign port."

'The plan was made. She left the palace secretly with a bag full of gold cups, and I, innocent child, went with her. But a few days into our voyage, the servant died suddenly on the ship. Her body was thrown to the fishes and I was left friendless. Later we came to Ithaca and Laertes bought me from the Phoenicians.'

'What a strange story of bad luck,' said Odysseus. 'I am sorry for your troubles. But you had good luck too, since you were bought by a kind master.'

Their conversation continued far into the night, until it was time to sleep. At the same time, Telemachus had had a lucky night. His ship was near the coast of Ithaca, and the crew had not seen the murderous suitors.

'Land on that beach,' he said to the men. 'I am going to get off there and visit my farms. Take the ship to the city without me.' He turned to one of the oarsmen, his loyal friend Peiraeus, and said, 'Could you give Theoclymenus a bed for the night? I will meet you in the city tomorrow.'

The crew took the ship onto the beach and Telemachus jumped out. He watched his companions as they sailed towards the city, then started along the path to Eumaeus's hut.

Eumaeus and Odysseus were preparing breakfast when Telemachus appeared in the doorway. Eumaeus jumped up in surprise, and the bowls in his hands fell noisily to the floor. He threw his arms around his young master like a loving father welcoming back his dear son after many years abroad.

'You are back, then, Telemachus! And I thought that I would never see you again after you sailed to Pylos. Come in, come in, dear child, and let me look at you. I do not see you often enough here on the farm.'

'It is good to see you too, Eumaeus. I have come here to ask for news from the palace. Is my mother still there, or has she married again and gone to her new husband's home?'

'She is still at the palace,' said the pig farmer. 'And she still spends most of her days in tears.'

Telemachus came into the hut, and Odysseus stood up to give him his seat. But Telemachus stopped him. 'Please, stranger, do not get up. I am sure that there is something else for me to sit on.'

Eumaeus made another seat of sticks and sheepskin, and Telemachus sat down next to his father, Odysseus. 'So who is your guest, Eumaeus?' he asked.

'He is from Crete,' replied the servant, 'but he cannot go back there. I am hoping that you can look after him at the palace.'

'The palace?' cried Telemachus. 'But how can I? My mother is usually too upset to receive visitors, and the suitors are a dangerous crowd. I can do little to protect him against so many. I am happy to give him food and new clothes. And I will send him wherever he wants to go. But while he is in Ithaca he should stay here with you. It will be safer for him here. But now, Eumaeus, old friend, can I ask you to take a message to my mother? Tell her that I am back from Pylos. Tell no one except her. There are many people who are trying to harm me.'

Eumaeus wasted no time. He left the hut immediately in the direction of the palace.

Athene saw him go. She appeared suddenly at the door of the hut, although only Odysseus could see her. Odysseus followed her outside, where she said, 'It is time to tell your son who you are. Together you must start planning the fate of those men in your palace.' As she spoke, she took away his disguise of old age. His strength and good looks returned; his beard grew dark on his chin; and he was wearing fine new clothes. Then the goddess disappeared, and Odysseus went back into the hut.

Telemachus looked at him now in wonder. 'Stranger, you look completely different. Only the gods can change their appearance in this way. Which god are you, and what can I do for you?'

'I am not a god,' replied Odysseus. 'But I *am* your father, who has been the cause of so many problems for you.'

He kissed his son, and tears ran down his face. But Telemachus stepped back from him. 'You are not my father,' he said. 'A god is playing a cruel trick on me. No man can change his appearance as you have just done.'

'I promise you that this is no trick. My disguise was the work of Athene, who has been a great help to me in my troubles.'

Telemachus was satisfied by this answer. He threw his arms around his father's neck. Together they cried tears of great sadness and great happiness. This was the moment that they had both dreamt about for so many years.

'But how did you get to Ithaca?' Telemachus asked finally.

'In a Phaeacian ship. I have a great pile of treasure, which is hidden in a cave by the beach. But we should waste no time. We must plan the death of those suitors. Tell me how many of them there are. Then I can decide how to fight them.'

'There are more than a hundred suitors. I know that you have a great reputation as a soldier, Father. But we cannot possibly fight them alone. We must think of some people who will fight with us.'

'Athene and Zeus will fight with us,' his father replied. 'Their help will be enough, I think.'

'If you are right, then the suitors have no chance,' Telemachus agreed.

'Tomorrow,' continued Odysseus, 'you will go back to the palace. I will join you later in the day, disguised again as an old man. If the suitors are rough with me, do not worry. Their day of judgement is coming. But tell no one about my return – not my father Laertes, or Eumaeus, or even your mother. It must be a complete secret until we have destroyed the suitors' power.'

'We must do that very soon, or Mother will marry one of them. Then it will be too late.'

As father and son discussed their plans, Telemachus's crew arrived at the port in the city. A messenger was sent to tell Penelope that her son was safe. This messenger arrived at the palace at the same time as Eumaeus, and soon gave the queen his message in front of all her servants. In private, Eumaeus told her everything that he knew. Then he went back to his farm – to Telemachus and Odysseus, who Athene had changed back into an old man.

The news of Telemachus's return soon spread to the suitors, who were very angry. When Antinous's ship came into port, they rushed to find out what had happened.

'The lucky young fool!' shouted Antinous. 'My people were looking for him all along the coast, but he managed to get past us. We must find another way to kill him, and do it fast. If we do not, he will call another meeting and turn the people of Ithaca against us. They will not be happy that we have tried to murder their prince. If we are not careful, we will soon be thrown off this island. We have no choice. We must kill him now, before it is too late.'

Silence followed this speech. Finally, Amphinomus stood up to speak. He was a more thoughtful man than the rest, one of the few suitors who Penelope liked to talk to. 'My friends,' he said now, 'I cannot agree to this murder. It is wrong to kill a prince, unless the gods have given clear signs that they want him dead. We should wait for those signs. Until then, we should do nothing.'

The other suitors agreed with him. For the moment, Telemachus was safe.

CHAPTER 10

Odysseus at the Palace

She quickly looked up at the stranger above her,
and she knew – her master had returned.

The next morning, Telemachus prepared to visit his mother at the palace. As he left Eumaeus's hut, he said to the pig farmer, 'After I have gone, take our visitor to the city. He can ask the people there for food.'

Telemachus met the prophet Theoclymenus in town, then walked with him to the palace. Loyal old Eurycleia was the first to see her young master, and she ran up to him with a cry of happiness. The other servants followed, and finally Penelope came out of her room. Tears ran down her face as she threw her arms around him. 'You are back, my child! And I thought I would never see you again after your secret departure. But come, tell me what you learnt on your voyage.'

'Well, we went first to Pylos. King Nestor received us kindly, but knew nothing about Odysseus's fate. He lent me a chariot, though, and with his son Peisistratus I went by land to Sparta and the palace of King Menelaus. During Menelaus's journey home from the war, he met the god Proteus. Proteus told him that my father was still alive, a prisoner on the goddess Calypso's island, without a ship or a crew to take him home.'

Telemachus's words warmed his mother's heart. Then his guest Theoclymenus added, 'Great Penelope, Menelaus's information is old. Listen to my prophecy. Your husband Odysseus is already in Ithaca, studying his enemies, the suitors, and planning their day of judgement.'

'I pray that you are right,' replied Penelope.

◆

Eumaeus and Odysseus were preparing to walk to the city. 'Are you sure you want to do this?' asked Eumaeus. 'The walk is not easy for a man of your age. Why not stay here in the hut instead?'

'Thank you, Eumaeus,' replied his guest. 'But your young master Telemachus is right. It is time for me to go. Could I ask you, though, for a stick to help me walk?'

Eumaeus got him a stick and they started their journey. The path was steep, but Odysseus went slowly and carefully and before long they came to a stream at the edge of the city. There they met Melanthius, who also looked after a farm on Odysseus's land. When this man saw Eumaeus, he immediately started shouting at him. 'Where are you going with that old ruin of a man? I hope you are not planning to take him to the palace. I doubt that he will manage a day in the suitors' company without broken bones. And the suitors are right too. He is a lazy fool who deserves nothing better.'

Melanthius then gave Odysseus a hard kick that almost knocked him over. As Odysseus was preparing to fight back, Eumaeus cried, 'Great Zeus, I pray that my master is returned to us. He would soon cure Melanthius of the arrogant ways that he has learnt from the suitors.'

Melanthius laughed as he walked away. 'Odysseus's chance of returning is as low as Telemachus's chance of escaping the suitors' violence. Things have changed, Eumaeus. You have new masters now.'

The pig farmer and the old man continued towards the palace. There was a dog called Argus lying near the gates. When he was younger, he had been an excellent hunting dog, trained by Odysseus himself and famous for his speed. But now he was old and lay all day in the dust, alone and forgotten. When this dog heard the sound of Odysseus's voice, he lifted his head and moved his tail in excitement. He did not have the strength to get up and greet his master. Odysseus saw his old hunting companion and gently touched the dog's head. At that same moment, Argus died – happy at last after waiting twenty years for his master's return.

Eumaeus went into the palace and joined Telemachus at the dinner in the hall. Odysseus followed a few minutes later and sat quietly in a dark corner. Seeing him there, Telemachus sent him a plate of food and an empty bag. Odysseus went from table to table, asking the suitors for food for his bag.

'I am a poor man,' he said to each man in the hall. 'Please, take pity on my hunger.' When the suitors saw the thin old man, most gave him food from their plate. But Antinous had other ideas. 'Who let this smelly old fool into the city? There are enough poor people on Ithaca already. How rude he is, asking for food when he offers nothing in return. You should throw him out of the palace, Telemachus.'

'Thank you for your advice,' replied Telemachus. 'You are very anxious not to let my food go to waste, I see! How can you be so greedy, Antinous? You have plenty on your plate. Give some of it to our guest.'

'I will do as I wish,' Antinous shouted back. He picked up a chair and threw it at Odysseus. It hit him hard on the shoulder. Telemachus managed to control his anger when he saw the attack. Odysseus, too, stayed calm. He looked around the hall at the suitors, saying, 'You are fortunate men, who know nothing about hunger. Does an empty stomach deserve this violent treatment? I hope that the gods are watching, and that Antinous will be dead before his wedding day.' Then he went back to sit on his chair in the corner of the hall.

The other suitors were shocked by Antinous's behaviour. Amphinomus spoke for them all when he said, 'This old man might be a god in disguise, Antinous. Be careful, or you will soon meet the fate that you deserve.' Amphinomus then

walked over to Odysseus and said, 'Your health, my friend! Fortune has not been kind to you recently, but I wish you a happy future.'

'Amphinomus,' Odysseus replied, 'you seem to be a sensible man. Why do you spend your days with these arrogant suitors? I have seen their violence and their greedy ways. And I know that Odysseus will soon be home. Listen to my advice, Amphinomus. Leave now and save yourself from Odysseus's bloody punishment.'

Amphinomus walked back to the table shakily, his mind full of doubt. Then he took some more meat and joined in the other suitors' conversation.

News of Antinous's attack on the stranger soon reached Penelope in her room. 'I hope that the gods strike Antinous as he struck that old man!' she cried to her servants. 'I hate all the suitors, but Antinous is even worse than the rest. He has a cold and cruel heart.'

She called Eumaeus to her so that she could ask about the stranger. When she learnt that he had travelled widely and had news of Odysseus, she wanted to question him herself. But she decided to wait until the suitors had gone home to their beds.

First, though, she wanted to talk to her son. 'It is not good for him to spend so much time in the company of those suitors,' she said to Eurycleia.

'You are right,' replied the servant. 'But you can be grateful, at least, that Telemachus has returned home safely and seems so grown up. It was always your greatest wish to see your son with a beard on his face.'

Penelope thought about her servant's words as she walked down to the hall. There, turning to her son, she said, 'Telemachus, you were always a sensible child, but now your good judgement has left you. Someone attacked an old man in this hall, and you did nothing to stop him! We are lucky that the stranger was not badly hurt.'

'Mother,' replied Telemachus, 'you are right to be upset. But I cannot always control the behaviour of your suitors. I am one against so many.'

Penelope now addressed the suitors. 'When my husband sailed to Troy, he warned me of the dangers that he would face. "I cannot promise that I will ever return," he said. "Wait patiently for me. But when you see a beard on our son's chin, it will be time for you to choose a new husband."

'Well, gentlemen, that time has come. I would prefer to die, but I must accept my fate. How, though, can I choose a husband, when none of my suitors behave correctly? Suitors usually bring their own animals to eat at dinners, and they also bring their lady gifts. They do not enjoy free meals given by their lady's own family.'

Antinous quickly replied, 'We will be happy to bring you presents, good lady. But we will not leave here – not until you have married one of us.'

The other suitors agreed. They sent servants to fetch the finest dresses and jewellery that they owned. Penelope accepted the gifts politely and took them to her room.

The suitors spent the rest of the day dancing and singing. But before darkness fell, Eurymachus started a conversation with Odysseus. 'Stranger,' he said, 'I could give you a job on my lands if you wanted. You could build walls and plant trees, and receive food and clothes in payment. But I doubt that you want an honest job. You prefer to get your food for nothing, you lazy dog!'

'What an insult!' replied Odysseus. 'We should have a competition, you and I. We could see who works harder – at building walls or digging fields, or any other work that you choose. Or would you prefer a swordfight? I could beat you in anything, you arrogant fool. You think you are a big man, a hero, but you have never had to face a *real* hero. If Odysseus returned now, you would soon run away in fear.'

Eurymachus was very angry. He took a chair and threw it at Odysseus. Odysseus stepped out of the way just in time, but it hit one of the servants. This man fell to the ground, dropping the wine cup that he was holding. There was a loud crash, and everyone started shouting.

Telemachus called out, 'What is wrong with you all this evening? Perhaps you have had too much wine. But it is late now. I suggest you all go home to your beds.'

The suitors were surprised by Telemachus's new confidence, but they followed his advice. Soon only Telemachus and his father were left in the hall.

Odysseus took advantage of their time alone. 'Quick, Telemachus,' he said. 'We must collect all the swords in the hall and hide them in an upstairs room. Leave only two swords here – one for you and one for me.'

'But what will I say if the suitors notice their absence?' asked Telemachus.

'Say that you are worried about their fights when they have drunk too much wine. You have taken the swords away for their own safety.'

When the swords were safely hidden, Telemachus went to bed. Penelope chose this quiet time of the evening to come down from her room and meet the stranger. Her servants came too, to clear the plates from the tables.

'Come and sit with me by the fire, stranger,' said Penelope. 'Tell me who you are and where you come from.'

'Please do not ask me about my home and family,' replied Odysseus. 'I have had a sad and difficult life. But no one likes to hear about other people's troubles. Let us talk about something else.'

'I, too, have had a sad and difficult life, stranger,' said Penelope. 'Since my husband's departure for the war in Troy, the passing years have brought me only tears. And now my father wants me to marry one of the men who behave so rudely in my home. But tell me about yourself. I would like to know your story.'

The old man repeated the story that he had told Eumaeus in his hut. When Penelope heard that he had once met Odysseus in Crete, she decided to test his honesty.

'Tell me, stranger, what Odysseus was like in those days. Can you remember any details of his clothes, or any companions that were with him?'

'It was twenty years ago, so I do not remember much. But I have not forgotten this: his clothes were a deep purple colour, and he also wore a gold pin with a picture of a dog on it. Everyone admired that pin. He had many companions, but he seemed closest to a man called Eurybates.'

Penelope was pleased with his answer. 'Friend, those were the clothes and the pin that I gave him when he left. But I will never again see the man who wore them.'

'Dear lady, do not upset yourself. I heard in Thesprotia that your husband was planning to sail here this week. For many years he was a prisoner far across the seas on Calypso's island, but now he is almost home. I promise you, he will be here very soon.'

'I hope that you are right, but I cannot believe it. In my heart I know that he will never return. But enough of this. The servants must get you a blanket. And Eurycleia, the oldest and best of them, will wash your feet.' She called to

Eurycleia. 'Come and help, old friend. Wash the dust from this man's aching feet. He once knew Odysseus, and has travelled far and wide. If Odysseus is still alive somewhere, his feet will be aching and dusty too.'

'Oh, Odysseus,' cried the servant as she fetched a bowl of water, 'the gods are so cruel! I looked after you as a baby, and still love you like a son. I want to be able to wash *your* feet, not the feet of a stranger.'

She sat at the stranger's feet to wash them, while Penelope gave instructions to the other servants. 'Old man,' said Eurycleia, 'we have had many travellers at the palace before, but none of them looked like Odysseus. You, though, have a very similar voice, and similar feet too …'

She started to wash his feet. As she passed her hands over his legs, she felt a **scar**. She remembered that Odysseus had had a scar in exactly the same place, from a hunting accident when he was a boy. She quickly looked up at the stranger above her, and she knew – her master had returned. She dropped his foot in shock, and it knocked over the bowl with a crash. But as the servant started to shout to Penelope, Odysseus put his hand over her mouth.

'Say nothing, dear Eurycleia,' he whispered. 'No one in the palace can know.'

'I will be as silent as a stone, my child,' she answered with a smile.

scar /skɑː/ (n) a mark on the skin that is left after an accident

6.1 Were you right?

Look at your answers to Activity 5.4. Then complete the sentences.

1 Odysseus first tells the news of his return to ....

2 .... recognises Odysseus from a scar on his leg.

3 .... and .... throw chairs at Odysseus.

6.2 What more did you learn?

Match the beginnings and endings of these sentences.

1 A prophet called Theoclymenus

2 Penelope

3 The farmer Melanthius

4 A dog called Argus

5 A suitor called Amphinomus

6 Eurymachus throws a chair, which

a dies when he knows that Odysseus has returned.

b wants to believe Theoclymenus's prophecy.

c hits a servant.

d is rude and violent.

e comes back from Pylos with Telemachus.

f talks kindly to Odysseus.

6.3 Language in use

Look at the sentences on the right.
Then write the correct verb forms in
these second conditional sentences.

> 'What **would** Menelaus **think** if we
> **rushed away** like thieves in the night?'
>
> 'If Odysseus **returned** now, you **would**
> soon **run away** in fear.'

1 Who ..... *would Penelope marry* ..... (Penelope marry) if Odysseus never
..... *returned* ..... (return)?

2 If Telemachus ..... (become) king, the suitors
..... (be) very angry.

3 Eurycleia ..... (not know) about Odysseus's return if
she ..... (not remember) his scar.

4 If Odysseus ..... (not be) in disguise, the suitors
..... (kill) him.

5 Antinous ..... (not behave) so rudely to Odysseus if he
..... (fear) the gods.

6.4 What happens next?

The next chapters are called 'The Day of Judgement' and 'Odysseus and
Penelope'. Which of these (✓) will be important, do you think? How? Make
notes.

Notes

| sheep | a bed | a bow | monsters |

| a tree | dresses | swords | a fire |

CHAPTER 11

The Day of Judgement

'The walls of this hall will be covered with your blood,
and screams of pain will fill the air.'

Odysseus could not sleep that night. He lay awake under the blanket that the servants had brought him, thinking angrily about the suitors. They deserved to die. But how could he and Telemachus alone kill so many?

Athene came down from Mount Olympus to talk to him. 'Are you sleepless again, Odysseus? Stop worrying! You are in your own home, under the same roof as your wife and son. And you have a goddess to help you. You and I could kill ten times this number of suitors. Their fate is already decided.'

Then she closed Odysseus's eyes in sleep and returned to Mount Olympus.

At the same moment, Penelope woke. In her dream, she had seen Odysseus next to her in bed. He was young and good-looking, as he had been on the day of his departure for Troy. The thought of him brought tears to her eyes. 'Oh gods,' she cried, 'let me die! A painful death would be better than marriage to any man who is not Odysseus.'

◆

In the morning, the palace was busy with preparations for a meal even bigger than usual. The day was a public holiday, and the suitors planned to celebrate it well.

Eumaeus arrived with some pigs for the meal, and the cow farmer Philoetius also brought some animals. When he saw Odysseus sitting quietly in a corner, he stopped suddenly and stared. 'Greetings, stranger,' he said. 'You confused me just then, because you reminded me so much of my master Odysseus. Oh, it would be a wonderful surprise if *he* ever came home. I often think of leaving Ithaca so that I do not have to obey the arrogant suitors' orders. But I cannot do it, because I cannot give up all hope of my master's return.'

Odysseus replied, 'You are clearly a loyal and honest servant, so I will give you some news. Odysseus is on his way home. Before the end of the day, you will see him again with your own eyes.'

'Stranger, I hope that you are right. It is my dearest wish.'

The farmer Melanthius, who had also come for the meal, heard their conversation. 'This smelly old man is mad, Philoetius,' he laughed. 'And you are mad too, if you listen to his crazy prophecies.'

When the food was ready, everyone took their seats in the hall. Telemachus carefully made sure that Odysseus was given a seat near the doorway. 'Sit and eat with the suitors,' he said loudly. 'Suitors, there will be no fights or insults here today.'

But they did not listen. Soon they were shouting and laughing at Odysseus. One of them threw a cow's foot at his head, but it missed. Telemachus turned to the man and said, 'You were lucky that that did not hit him. I will put my sword through any man who strikes my guest. I am not a child now. I cannot stop you eating my food and drinking my wine – there are too many of you. But I *will* stop your bad behaviour. If you want to murder me for that, then do it. I would prefer to die than to let you hurt my guest.'

The suitors laughed at his words, until they saw strange drops of blood on their food. Was this a sign from the gods?

At that moment, the voice of the prophet Theoclymenus was heard. 'Unhappy men,' he cried, 'this is my prophecy. The walls of this hall will be covered with your blood, and screams of pain will fill the air. Your ghosts will soon be on their way to the Underworld.'

Eurymachus laughed at him. 'He is out of his mind, poor man. Can someone show him the door?'

'I need no help to find the door, Eurymachus,' replied Theoclymenus. 'I am going through it now. I can see disaster coming your way, and I want to be as far from you as possible when it arrives.'

He left the hall. The suitors looked at each other nervously, but then started to laugh again. 'You have chosen some strange people to invite here as your guests, Telemachus,' said one. 'First a smelly old man, and now a mad prophet.'

At this point Penelope entered the hall. She had spent the morning thinking sadly about her situation. Now she had reached a decision.

'Suitors,' she said, 'you have taken advantage of my son for long enough. Although I have no wish to marry again, I must now choose a new husband. That is the only way to save my son's property from your greedy hands. Today will be the last day that you eat free food in this palace. Tomorrow I will go to the home of my chosen husband, and the rest of you will leave this place.

'As you can see, I am carrying a bow. This belonged to my husband, the famous hero Odysseus. I will marry the man among you who is most skilled at using this bow. You must string it, which is not easy if you do not have Odysseus's great strength. And then you must shoot an arrow through twelve **axe** handles. Telemachus, please arrange the axes in a line.'

Telemachus took the axes that his mothers' servants were carrying. He dug the axe heads into the ground, so that the metal rings on the handles were exactly in line. Then he said, 'Gentlemen, you have your instructions for the competition. But before you start, I would like to try the bow myself. Tomorrow I will have

axe /æks/ (n) a tool with a long handle and a flat piece of sharp metal at the end, used in war and for cutting trees

to say goodbye to my mother. But if I succeed with the bow, at least I will know that I am as strong as my father.'

Telemachus stood in the doorway with the bow. Three times he tried to bend it, but three times his strength failed. The bow shook but it did not bend. He tried a fourth time and felt that he would succeed. But Odysseus shook his head gently and Telemachus put the bow back on the ground.

'Well, clearly I will always be known as a weak man compared to my father,' he said. 'This bow is too much for me. Who else will try it?'

Leodes was the first suitor to come forward. He tried and tried to bend the bow, but it was impossible. 'Friends, I cannot do it,' he said. 'Let someone else try. But I fear that this bow will break the heart of many men here today.'

Antinous cried, 'Do you think that you are the strongest man in the room, Leodes? *You* cannot string the bow, but others will do it. Wait and see.'

Other men tried, but they failed too. Eurymachus and Antinous watched and waited, learning from the others' mistakes.

At this point Eumaeus and Philoetius the cow farmer left the hall. The competition was bringing to an end their hopes for Odysseus's happy return. They could not watch it any longer.

But Odysseus came running after them. 'My friends,' he said, 'do not leave yet. I have an important question for you. If Odysseus returned, would you fight with him, or with the suitors?'

'You would soon see the strength of my right arm if I could fight the suitors at Odysseus's side!' Philoetius replied. Eumaeus agreed enthusiastically.

Odysseus continued, 'Well, here I am! Yes, it is true – I am your master, returned at last. Look, here is the scar that I got in a hunting accident as a boy.'

As he spoke, he showed them his leg. When they saw the scar, the farmers threw their arms around their master and tears ran down their faces.

'Stop crying,' said Odysseus, 'or someone will see us. Now, I need your help. Come back inside and wait until I have the bow in my hands. Then, Philoetius, go and lock the palace gate. Eumaeus, you must lock the door to the women's rooms. Tell the servants not to listen to any noises that they hear in the hall.'

They went back inside and continued to watch the suitors with the bow. It was now Eurymachus's turn. He was a proud man, used to success in all things. He tried again and again to string the bow, but it refused to bend. Finally, he cried out in anger, 'Stupid bow! This is bad news for all of us. I do not care about the marriage – there are plenty of other rich women. But all over Greece, people will say that we are weak compared to the great Odysseus.'

'Everything will be fine, Eurymachus,' said Antinous. 'Today is a public holiday – a day for fun, not for tests of strength. Let us leave the competition for now. Tomorrow we will pray to the god Apollo, whose skill with the bow is famous among gods and men. Then we will try our strength again.'

The other suitors liked this idea. But Odysseus stood up and said, 'Before you stop, could I try? I would like to see if there is any strength left in these old arms of mine.'

The suitors were very angry. They were frightened that the strange old man would succeed where they had failed.

'If you touch that bow, stranger, we will take you prisoner and sell you abroad,' said Antinous. 'We will …'

Penelope interrupted him. 'Antinous, stop. This poor stranger is our guest, and you must talk to him politely. He has no intention of becoming my husband. I am sure he knows that that is impossible. So let him try his strength against the rest of you. What harm could it do?'

It was Eurymachus who replied. 'The people will think badly of us if he succeeds. He is old and homeless, and we are the finest young men in Greece. Our reputations will be ruined!'

Penelope gave a little laugh. 'For years you have been eating and drinking, uninvited, at another man's table. Your reputations were ruined long ago, Eurymachus.'

'Mother,' said Telemachus, 'the bow was my father's, so now it is mine. *I* should choose who can hold it. But go now to your room and busy yourself with your work. Or sleep if you can – you look tired today. The competition to choose your husband will start again tomorrow.'

Penelope realised that Telemachus was right. She left the hall and returned to her bedroom. There, tired after her sleepless night, she fell asleep.

Telemachus now ordered Eumaeus to take the bow to Odysseus. The suitors shouted insults at the pig farmer, but Eumaeus did as Telemachus said. When he had given Odysseus the bow, he went up to the women's rooms and locked the doors. At the same time, Philoetius went out quietly and locked the palace gate. Now there was no escape for the suitors.

Odysseus was looking carefully at the bow, to see if the passing years had damaged it. When he was satisfied that it was as strong as before, he started to bend it. As easily as a bard strings his instrument before a musical performance, Odysseus bent the bow and put on the string. As the suitors looked at him angrily, they heard thunder outside. Odysseus smiled at this sign of support from the great god Zeus.

He picked up an arrow, aimed and shot. He did not miss a single ring. The arrow sped straight through from the first axe handle to the last.

Odysseus looked at Telemachus to check that he had his sword ready. Then he said, 'Suitors, I have won your competition. But now I am going to shoot

something that no one has ever hit before.' From the doorway, he aimed an arrow at Antinous.

Antinous had just reached for his wine cup. He never imagined for one moment that anyone would try to kill him in the company of so many friends. The arrow hit him in the neck. The cup dropped from his hand and he fell to the floor with a crash.

The suitors stared at Antinous's dead body in shock. 'Stranger,' they shouted, 'you will pay for this accident with your blood.' Many of them were not carrying their swords, so they looked for the swords on the walls. Too late, they realised that the swords had disappeared. They still had no idea who the stranger was, and believed that Antinous's death had been a horrible mistake.

Odysseus cried, 'You dogs! You never thought that I would come back from Troy. So you stole my food. Then you tried to steal my wife and murder my son. For those crimes, you will all die.'

The suitors' faces turned white with fear, and they looked around for somewhere to hide. Only Eurymachus was brave enough to speak. 'If you really are Odysseus, then you are right to be angry. But the person responsible for those crimes lies dead already. Antinous was power-hungry and cruel. He wanted to make himself King of Ithaca after killing your son – but he has paid the price. The rest of us are guilty of nothing except eating your food without permission. For this we will each give you twenty cows and a generous repayment in gold. Think carefully, Odysseus, before you murder innocent men.'

'Eurymachus,' replied Odysseus, 'no amount of gold could pay for your crimes. You have only two choices – to fight or to run. But whatever you choose, you will soon be dead.'

Eurymachus called to the other suitors, 'Odysseus will not be stopped with words. Get your swords ready, men. We must fight!'

Eurymachus ran at Odysseus with his sword, but Odysseus shot an arrow at his chest. He fell across the table, knocking food and wine cups everywhere before lying, dead, in a pool of blood. Amphinomus came straight after him. Telemachus killed him from behind as he ran at Odysseus.

'Father,' shouted Telemachus, 'I will go and get some swords for Eumaeus and Philoetius.'

'Yes,' replied Odysseus. 'But do it quickly. When I have no more arrows, I will need help.'

Telemachus got swords for the two loyal servants. Odysseus shot arrow after arrow, and each one brought death to a suitor. When there were no more arrows, he took his sword and fought with his son and servants at his side.

The suitors, with few swords between them, could do little to defend themselves. But Melanthius the farmer had an idea. 'Telemachus must have the swords from the hall somewhere in the palace. I know the building well. I will go and look for them.'

He came back a few minutes later with an armful of swords. Then he went back to get more. With new confidence, the suitors threw themselves at Odysseus and his companions in the doorway. Suddenly, Odysseus felt less sure that they could win against so many.

'Where are they getting the swords from?' he asked his son. 'Who in the palace is helping them?'

'Look!' cried Eumaeus. 'Melanthius has a great pile of swords. He has found the room where they are hidden. He has given them to the suitors, and is going to get more.'

'Telemachus and I will keep the suitors in the hall,' Odysseus said to Eumaeus. 'Go now with Philoetius and stop Melanthius.'

Odysseus's loyal servants went in the same direction as Melanthius. They found him getting more swords from Telemachus's secret room. They jumped on him before he saw them and he was dead when they ran back to the hall.

The suitors were now fighting hard, but Odysseus and Telemachus had managed to keep them from the doorway. At this point, Athene came to them disguised as Odysseus's old friend Mentor. 'Mentor!' cried Odysseus, guessing that he was really speaking to the goddess, 'you have come at just the right moment. Will you fight with us?'

'You were braver when you were fighting the Trojans' finest soldiers,' she replied. 'Now you are in your own home, against a group of lazy fools. You do not need me to fight with you, Odysseus.'

She changed into a bird and flew high above the men's heads to watch the fight. The suitors started to attack in groups of six. But Athene made sure that their swords could not hurt Odysseus and his companions. As their attacks failed again and again, the suitors' confidence left them. Finally, they ran to hide where they could. Odysseus and his men ran after them and cut them down without pity. The suitors screamed horribly as they died, and the floor was a lake of blood.

Phemius the bard looked around in terror. He felt sure that he was going to die with the suitors. But his only crime had been to entertain them with his songs. He ran to Odysseus and threw his arms around the hero's knees. 'Sir,' he cried, 'take pity on me. You will be sorry later if you kill a bard. My songs bring pleasure to both gods and men. Your son, Telemachus, can tell you – I did not choose to come here. I was forced here by the suitors.'

'It is true, Father,' said Telemachus. 'The man is innocent.'

'Then go outside to safety,' Odysseus said to Phemius. 'I have more work to do in here.'

When the bard had gone, Odysseus looked round the hall for more suitors to kill. But they were all piled on the floor on top of each other. No one was left alive.

CHAPTER 12

Odysseus and Penelope

As she walked towards the hall, Penelope could not decide how to greet him. Should she be polite but cold, or should she run into his arms and kiss him?

Odysseus now said to Telemachus, 'Go and fetch Eurycleia and the other servants. We must clean up the mess.'

The servants came out of their rooms and learnt what had happened. They threw their arms around Odysseus to welcome him home. He greeted each one by name, trying to keep the tears from his eyes.

When they had taken the suitors' bodies outside and washed away the blood in the hall, Odysseus said, 'Tomorrow I will visit my father. But now, Eurycleia, it is time to fetch Penelope.'

'Dear child,' replied the servant, 'you should first change your clothes. It is not right for the King of Ithaca to be dressed in dirty bits of cloth.'

'No,' said Odysseus, 'I have waited twenty years for this moment. I will not wait a minute longer.'

So Eurycleia hurried upstairs to wake Penelope. She almost fell over her own feet in her excitement to tell the news. 'Penelope, my dear, wake up!' she cried. 'Come and see the sight that you have prayed for all these years. Odysseus is home at last, and he has killed every one of the suitors.'

'Have the gods driven you mad, Eurycleia?' replied Penelope. 'Please, do not make fun of my unhappiness. Go back downstairs and let me sleep some more.'

'But I am not making fun of you, dear child,' the servant continued. 'Odysseus really has come home. He is the stranger who the suitors insulted in the hall.'

Penelope's heart jumped inside her chest. She rushed out of bed and held Eurycleia in her arms, with tears running down her face.

'Eurycleia, can it really be true? And how did he manage to kill all the suitors without an army to help him?'

'I did not see anything, and I was not told anything, but from my room I heard the cries of dying men. Then Telemachus called me and the other servants into the hall, and we saw Odysseus standing among the dead bodies. We have cleaned up the mess, and now Odysseus wants to see you. Come now and welcome him home.'

'You believe too easily, dear Eurycleia. There is something strange about this story. I feel sure that the gods are trying to trick us. Perhaps the man in the hall is a god in disguise.'

'But I saw his scar – you know, the one that he got in a hunting accident.'

'Eurycleia, you are a wise woman, but even you cannot see into the hearts and minds of the gods. But come, I am glad that the suitors are dead. I will talk to the man who killed them.'

As she walked towards the hall, Penelope could not decide how to greet him. Should she be polite but cold, or should she run into his arms and kiss him? When she saw the man by the fire, she just stared at his face in confusion. At times she saw her husband's face there, but at other times he looked to her like a stranger.

'Mother,' said Telemachus crossly, 'why are you not welcoming my father home?'

'I am sorry, my son,' she replied. 'The shock has turned my tongue to stone. I cannot say a word to him.'

Odysseus now said, 'Telemachus, I need to wash, and then your mother and I need some time alone. Go and organise a dance for the servants. And do not worry. Everything will be fine.'

While Telemachus asked Phemius for some music, Odysseus had a bath and put on some fine new clothes. Then Athene worked her magic on his appearance, giving him a younger face and a stronger body. When he went back to Penelope in the hall, he looked like a god.

'Well, Penelope, you are a strange woman. Few wives would stay out of their husbands' arms for as long as this. But I can wait. Eurycleia, please prepare a bed for me somewhere in the palace. I will be sleeping alone tonight.'

'*You* seem a strange *man* to me too. All these years I have carried a picture of you in my head. But you do not look like that picture. Come, Eurycleia, we must move the great bed that Odysseus himself built. Take it outside the bedroom and make it comfortable for him.'

This was Penelope's test for the man in front of her. He replied angrily, 'Lady, your words are like a knife in my heart. What have you done to our bed? I built it myself, using a tree that was growing in the palace as one of the bed's legs. No one can move it – unless you have cut through the wood of the tree and destroyed it.'

At these words, Penelope's knees began to shake. No one knew the secret of the tree-bed except her husband and a servant who had died many years before.

'Do not be angry with me, Odysseus,' she cried. 'The bed is exactly as you left it. But I was so frightened that someone would come here pretending to be you. This was my test – and now I know. Husband, it is really you!'

She threw her arms around him. She was like a sailor whose ship has been destroyed in a storm. After swimming for many hours, he sees dry land and knows that he is saved. Penelope felt the same way about seeing her husband again. For a long time Odysseus and Penelope held each other, crying silently.

When everyone else in the palace had gone to bed, Odysseus finally broke the silence. 'Dear wife, we have not yet come to the end of our troubles. On my journey home, I spoke with the prophet Teiresias. He told me that I had to make another long journey before I could enjoy a peaceful old age.'

Penelope questioned her husband about the details of this prophecy. 'If the gods have promised you a more peaceful old age,' she said finally, 'then there is hope that one day our troubles will end.'

Odysseus smiled at her words. Then he took his dear wife to their bed.

1 Imagine that you are Odysseus and Penelope, and you are together again after twenty years. Talk about your lives since you last saw each other.

2 Discuss which character from the story each of these adjectives best describes. Why does the adjective fit the character?

resourceful	arrogant	loyal	selfish	cruel

3 Discuss what Odysseus did in these situations. If you were in his position, would you behave in a similar way? What would you do differently?

A

B

C

D

Complete this letter from Odysseus to his friend Menelaus.

Dear Menelaus

I am home at last! My journey was very difficult.
I_____
_____
_____
_____

The situation was difficult when I first arrived in
Ithaca too. There were _____
_____
_____

I had to _____
_____
_____

Everything is fine now, although I must soon _____
_____
_____

I am so sorry to hear _____
_____
_____

Thank you for looking after _____
_____

I hope that we can meet again soon.
Best wishes

Odysseus

WORK IN GROUPS OF THREE OR FOUR.

1 Imagine that you are sailors at the time that Odysseus was alive. Make a list of things that you might have on your ship.

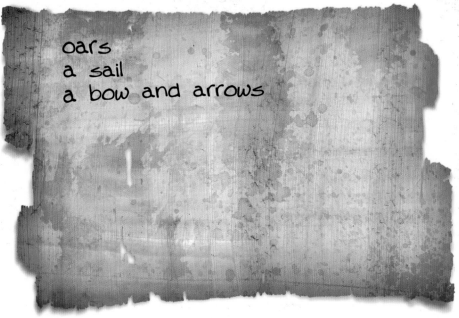

oars
a sail
a bow and arrows

2 You are caught in a storm. Your ship has been destroyed, and you have to swim to the nearest island. Choose one thing from the ship that each of you will take with you.

....

....

....

....

....

....

3 You arrive safely on the island with your things from the ship. No one lives on the island. Decide which one of these you find there.

☐ a stream ☐ a cave ☐ a lake ☐ fruit trees ☐ sheep

4 Now read about Daniel Foss, who was in a similar situation, but was alone. Discuss how he:

a found food
b got fresh water
c stayed warm and dry
d tried to make contact with passing ships

In 1810, American sailor Daniel Foss's boat was destroyed on the rocky coast of a Pacific island. He held onto an oar and swam to shore. He was the only person on the boat to arrive safely on land. For a week he could find no food on the island, which was less than a kilometre from end to end. Then he discovered a beach with hundreds of seals on it. He used his oar to kill some of the seals and their meat gave him back his strength. He made stone buckets to collect rainwater by hitting a big stone with a small stone repeatedly for weeks and weeks. Then he built a stone hut. At the highest point on the island, he made a pile of stones ten metres high, with his red shirt on the top to get the attention of any passing ships. He kept a diary on the only flat piece of wood on the island – his oar. He cut into it with a sharp stone and managed to write twelve letters a day.

After five years on the island, Foss saw a ship. He jumped into the sea and swam to the ship, helped by his oar. This amazing oar was once a popular sight in America, but sadly no one knows if it still exists.

5 Look back at your answers to Activities 2 and 3. Discuss how you will stay alive on your island.

Jobs

6 Five years later, a ship finally arrives and you can leave the island! A student from another group is the sailor who saved you. Talk about your experience.

- Why were you on the island without a boat?
- How long were you there?
- How did you manage to stay alive?
- What was life like for you on the island?
- How do you feel now?